Gadamer on Celan

SUNY Series in Contemporary Continental Philosophy
Dennis J. Schmidt, Editor

Gadamer on Celan

"Who Am I and Who Are You?"
and other essays

Hans-Georg Gadamer

translated and edited by

Richard Heinemann and Bruce Krajewski
with an Introduction by Gerald L. Bruns

State University of New York Press

Wer bin Ich und wer bist Du?: Ein Kommentar zu Paul Celans Gedichtfolge "Atemkristall" by Hans-Georg Gadamer reprinted with permission of Suhrkamp Verlag © 1973, 1986

"Sinn und Sinnverhüllung bei Paul Celan" by Hans-Georg Gadamer appears in *POETICA: Ausgewählte Essays,* reprinted with permission by Insel Verlag © 1977

"Phänomenologischer und semantischer Zugang zu Celan?" by Hans-Georg Gadamer first appeared in *Paul Celan "Atemwende": Materialen,* edited by Gerhard Buhr und Roland Reuss, and is reprinted with permission by Verlag Könighausen & Neumann © 1991, and by permission of the publishers of Gadamer's *Gesammelte Werke,* J. C. B. Mohr (Paul Siebeck) © 1993

Published by
State University of New York Press, Albany

© 1997 State University of New York

For information, address State University of New York Press,
State University Plaza, Albany, N.Y., 12246

Production by Marilyn P. Semerad
Marketing by Dana E. Yanulavich

Library of Congress Cataloging-in-Publication Data

Gadamer, Hans Georg, 1900–
    [Wer bin ich und wer bist du? English]
    Gadamer on Celan : "Who am I and who are you?" and other essays / Hans-Georg Gadamer ; translated and edited by Richard Heinemann and Bruce Krajewski ; with an introduction by Gerald L. Bruns.
      p. cm. — (SUNY series in contemporary continental philosophy)
    Includes index.
    ISBN 0-7914-3229-7 (alk. paper). — ISBN 0-7914-3230-0 (pbk. : alk. paper)
    1. Celan, Paul—Criticism and interpretation. I. Heinemann, Richard, 1962– . II. Krajewski, Bruce, 1959– . III. Title. IV. Series.
PT2605.E4Z61613   1997
831'.914—dc21
                                         96-39208
                                          CIP

10 9 8 7 6 5 4 3 2 1

Contents

The Remembrance of Language: An Introduction to Gadamer's Poetics

Gerald L. Bruns

My dear Degas, one does not make poetry with ideas, but with words.
—*Mallarmé*

The continual pausing for breath is the mode most proper to the process of contemplation.
—*Walter Benjamin*

At first glance Gadamer's commentary on the "Atemkristall" of Paul Celan seems unprepossessing: a deeply personal but slender and mildly impressionistic response to a thin sheaf of very short poems. This is certainly what it is, and as such it lacks the sweep and dramatic gesture of *Schibboleth*, Jacques Derrida's text on Celan that has come to have such a strong influence on the reception of Celan, particularly in the United States. Nevertheless, for all of its simplicity, and possibly because of it, *Wer bin Ich und wer bist Du?* is the centerpiece of Gadamer's most important philosophical project since the publication of *Wahrheit und Methode* (1960). Put simply, the purpose of this project is to address the claims of aesthetic modernity. How are we to understand Marcel Duchamp's provocation when he exhibits a snow shovel in his studio and declares it to be his most recent composition? Why isn't this just nonsense? How is it that a movement like Cubism, for example, or Schoenberg's twelve-tone music, or the hermetic lyric inaugurated by Mallarmé's *poésie pure*, can exert a claim on us as powerful and authoritative as that of the classic or traditional work of art, or what Gadamer likes to call

1

"the eminent text"?[1] What is the nature of this claim, and how can one who is no longer a modernist—or who perhaps has never been modern, say a classical philologist—respond to it? What sort of response is called for?

I would like to engage this question in some detail. Part of what is at stake is certainly the famous "hermeneutical claim to universality." In "Ästhetik und Hermeneutik" (1964) Gadamer says that "The hermeneutical perspective is so comprehensive . . . that it must even include the experience of beauty in nature and art" (GW8.1/PH96). It follows that it must include aesthetic modernity as well. But modernist art is a considerable challenge to hermeneutical universality because so much of it—Duchamp's readymades, for example—is outside the "experience of beauty." It is even outside art and, to all appearances, outside intelligibility. What makes Gadamer's project interesting is that the issue here is not just the logical problem of making hermeneutics coherent with itself. He understands, as perhaps Heidegger (for example) did not, that the claims of modernity cannot be brushed aside with a superior gesture. He seems genuinely fascinated by Duchamp. But both the claims of twentieth-century art and our responsibility to it are in need of clarification, and this is the purpose of Gadamer's project, part of which includes, of course, a reconceptualization of aesthetics (and of beauty) to include what cannot be comprehended within the limits of intelligibility.

The Corporeality of Language

One can make these matters conceptually more precise. Gadamer's writings on poetry and aesthetics since 1960 are an attempt to come to philosophical terms with the radical thesis of modern poetry—what Gadamer thinks of as *lyric* modernity—namely the idea that a poem is made of words, not of images or meanings.[2] The classic defense of this thesis perhaps belongs to Paul Valéry, to whom Gadamer frequently refers and whose characterization of poetic language seems to some extent decisive for him. In an essay on "The Poet's Rights Over Language" (1927), for example, Valéry writes:

Ordinary spoken language is a practical tool. It is constantly resolving immediate problems. Its task is fulfilled when each sentence has been completely abolished, annulled, and replaced by the meaning. Comprehension is its end. But on the other hand poetic usage is dominated by personal conditions, by a conscious, continuous, and sustained musical feeling.

Here language is no longer a transitive act, an expedient. On the contrary, it has its own value, which must remain intact in spite of the operations of the intellect on the given propositions. Poetic language must preserve itself, through itself, and remain the same, not to be altered by the act of intelligence that finds or gives it a meaning.[3]

A poem is made of language but is not a use of it, that is, it is not constituted by any of the things that language can be used to produce—concepts, propositions, intentional fulfillments, descriptions of the world, expressions of subjectivity, and so on. However one figures it, the language of poetry is irreducible or excessive with respect to its function. In poetry language is no longer (or no longer simply) a form of mediation. However possible it is to analyze a poem or a work of art according to semantic or representational categories—and, of course, we hardly know what else to do—one very quickly encounters a limit, as if the poem were withdrawing into its words. The poem, Gadamer says, is "language-bound *[sprachgebunden]*," in contrast to "intentional speech [which] points away from itself" (GW8.21/RB69). But what does this mean, exactly? Gadamer says that the whole effort of his thought has been "directed toward not forgetting the limit *[Grenze]* that is implicit in every hermeneutical experience of meaning" (GW2.334/DD25). What sort of limit—or "limit experience"—is this (as if it were just one)?[4]

In order to understand, not just Gadamer, but what Gadamer is getting at, we need to discriminate among several answers to this question. According to structuralist poetics, for example, poetry is defamiliarized, foregrounded, or self-referential language.[5] This is not wrong, but it is not always carefully understood. Jürgen Habermas, for example, thinks of poetry as a foregrounding of the "rhetorical elements" of language at the expense of the "normal," problem-solving mechanisms of communicative action.[6] Habermas wants to retain the Kant-like idea of the poem as an aesthetic object set apart from science, morality, and everyday life. The task of criticism and, at a higher level, of philosophy (conceived once more as "the guardian of rationality") is to translate poetry back into the practical discourse of the lifeworld.[7] But it is precisely the possibility of such a translation that the radical thesis of modern poetry calls into question. What is the meaning of poetry's resistance to such translation? Is this resistance merely "aesthetic" in the sense in which Habermas understands this term—namely, the expression of the autonomy of the work of art with respect to the social, political, and ethical demands of everyday life? Is poetry simply a species of sealed-off linguistic formalism?

Structuralist poetics tends to flatten out the radical thesis just to the extent that it thinks of poetry as an aestheticization of language. But aestheticization of language is not how most poets think of it. In *Spring and All* (1923), to take an illustrious example, William Carlos Williams summed up the radical thesis as follows: "Of course it must be understood that writing deals with words and words only and that all discussions of it deal with single words and their associations in groups."[8] However, Williams (under the direct influence of Duchamp, but also perhaps that of Gertrude Stein) interpreted this thesis in an explicitly non-aesthetic way, one that has become foundational for some of the most important contemporary movements in North American and European poetry. Valéry, following Mallarmé, thinks of poetic language as separate from ordinary speech, whereas the Williams tradition thinks of poetry as internal to the discourse of everyday life, as if there were nothing unpoetic about the ordinary.[9] The poet is simply one who listens to the language of his or her environment and responds to it—doesn't try to reduce it or objectify it as so many surface structures or speech acts, so much *parole* or *Gerede*. In *Kora in Hell* (1920) Williams writes:

> *That which is heard from the lips of those to whom we are talking in our day's affairs mingles with what we see in the streets and everywhere about us as it mingles*

also with our imaginations. By this chemistry is fabri-cated a language of the day which shifts and reveals its meaning as clouds shift and turn in the sky and some-times send down rain or snow or hail. This is the lan-guage to which few ears are tuned so that it is said by poets that few men are ever in their full senses since they have no way to use their imaginations. Thus to say that a man has no imagination is to say nearly that he is blind or deaf. But of old poets would translate this hidden language into a kind of replica of the speech of the world within certain distinctions of rhyme and meter to show that it was not really that speech. Nowadays the elements of that language are set down as heard and the imagination of the listener and of the poet are left free to mingle in the dance. (Imaginations, p. 59)

The "hidden" language that the poets bring out into the open is not a transcendental language of the gods; it is not anything occult, subterranean, or otherworldly (not Walter Benjamin's "pure language—which no longer means or expresses anything but, as expressionless and creative Word, that which is meant in all languages").[10] It is only the quotidian speech of ordinary mortals, language in all its human facticity, the word in everyone's mouth. Poetry—in particular, *modern* poetry—is not the speaking of an aesthetically differentiated language. Possibly one could say it is not a kind of speaking at all but a kind of listening or attunement to the linguisticality of human everydayness: "*language set down as heard.*" "A poem can be made of anything," Williams says (*Imaginations*, p. 70)—even of newspaper clippings, as if a poem (like a work of art by Duchamp) could be found ready-to-hand. The poem is in this sense non-aesthetic; it doesn't have to be "poetical" to be poetic.[11]

This conception of poetry as a listening to the language of the everyday environment—to language as a *social fact*—is a basic principle of contemporary European and North American poetics. The American poet Ron Silliman puts it as bluntly as one can: "there is no useful distinction between language and poetry."[12] Poetry is language—language which hasn't been tuned out, re-pressed, forgotten, or processed by the semantic, propositional, or representational operations of the spirit. As Silliman likes to say, poetry is unconsumed and unconsumable language.[13] Gadamer has grasped this principle exactly: "what makes understanding possible is precisely the forgetfulness of language *[Sprachver-gessenheit]*, a forgetting of the formal elements in which the discourse or text is encased" ("Text und Interpretation," GW2.342/ DD32). Whence it follows that poetry is simply *the remembrance of language*. The truth of poetry consists in this remembrance.

Notice what this means. The radical thesis is that poetry is an event that takes place at the limits of intelligibility defined by the remembrance of language. It is *not* a thesis that poetry is unintelligible. In an essay on "Philosophy and Poetry" (1977), Gadamer asks about "the ontological constitution of poetic language" (GW8.235/RB134). As the limiting case of *poésie pure* shows, poetic language is not a form of mediation but stands on its own. "The structuring of sound, rhyme, rhythm, intonation, assonance, and so on, furnishes the stabilizing factors that haul back and bring to a standstill the fleeting word that points beyond itself." In poetry "the word speaks as word" (GW8.49). The poetic word is self-standing *[Selbstständlich]*: it withdraws from its function as a sign. It is constituted (not just formally but ontologically) by its materiality—or, as Gadamer prefers, its "corporeality *[Sprachlich-Leibhaften]*" (WM153/TM160). Materiality or corporeality here need not be restricted to sonority; as Maurice Blanchot says of poetic language: "Everything physical takes precedence: rhythm, weight, mass, shape, and then the paper on which one writes, the trail of ink, the book."[14] In any event the point, as Gadamer says, is that poetic language is still language: the "logico-grammatical forms of intelligible speech" are not replaced by non-words (GW8.235/RB135). It is only that these forms no longer annihilate the corporeality of language in order to achieve the purity or transparency of the sign. Hence the appeal of Valéry's idea that "the value of a poem resides in the indissolubility of sound and sense" (*The Art of Poetry*, p. 74). In poetry, language, as Gadamer says, stands on its own and does not give way to anything else: it is irreducible to its signification. "The consequent ambiguity and obscurity of the text may be the despair of the interpreter, but it is a structural element of this kind of poetry" (GW8.235/RB135).

But perhaps it were better to say simply that in poetry the uncanniness—the strangeness, the exteriority—of ordinary language brings us up short, *even in the moments of its plainness and unmistakable intelligibility and meaning.* It is not that poetry renders language ambiguous, obscure, or unintelligible in itself (as if turning it into gibberish or nonsense—Gadamer is particularly wary of reducing poetry to word-play or the rhetorical manipulation of words: Mallarmé is not Edward Lear). Rather it is that poetry alters our relation to language. Poetry is an event—Gadamer calls it a "speculative" event—in which language interrupts our attempts to reduce it conceptually and instrumentally; it takes itself out of our hands.[15] The poet Michael Davidson gives us a very simple, straightforward, undramatic and unambiguous account of this basic poetic phenomenon (an event, as Davidson tells it, that makes the poet):

> I have a kind of naive idea of what a fact is. To paraphrase Wittgenstein, it's a point of departure for further investigation. I think it began with my interest in lists. At one point the idea of a list was a sort of ultimate autistic construct, because it would create the illusion of a random series that would relate immediately to my life. I would be able to go through my day and check off items on the list. They were words after all, but the syntax of the list was my activity [i.e., my daily life]. In that sense, it was a hermeneutic of reading the list. And then I began to realize that I wanted to tell stories; I wanted to describe events. And the problem, of course, occurred in the first few words: as I began to describe the event I was faced with my own language staring me back in the face. I simply couldn't describe. I found myself involved in the forms of mediation that were constantly coming up in front of me.[16]

One can fruitfully compare this to Stanley Cavell's analysis of ordinary language, apropos of Edgar Poe's story, "The Imp of the Perverse," a text strangely (if unobviously) overloaded with what Cavell calls "imp-words"—"*impulse* (several times), *impels* (several times), *impatient* (twice), *important, impertinent, imperceptible, impossible, unimpressive, improvised,* and, of course, *Imp.* More-over *imp,* is an abbreviation in English for *imperative, imperfect, imperial, import, imprimatur, impersonal, implement, improper, and improvement."* What is it to experience "word imps"?

> "Word imps" could name any of the recurrent combina-
> tions of letters of which the words of a language are
> composed. They are part of the way words have their
> familiar looks and sounds, and their familiarity depends
> upon our mostly not noticing the particles (or cells) and
> their laws, which constitute words and imps—on our
> not noticing their necessary recurrences, which is per-
> haps only to say that recurrence constitutes familiarity.
> This necessity, the most familiar property of language
> there could be—that if there is to be language, words
> and their cells must recur, as if fettered in their orbits,
> that language is grammatical (to say the least)—insures
> the self-referentiality of language. When we do note
> these cells or molecules, these little moles of language
> (perhaps in thinking, perhaps in derangement), what we
> discover are word imps—the initial, or it may be medial
> or final, movements, the implanted origins or constitu-
> ents of words, leading lives of their own, staring back
> at us, calling upon one another, giving us away, alarm-
> ing—because to note them is to see that they live in
> front of our eyes, within earshot, at every moment. (*In
> Quest of the Ordinary,* pp. 124–25)

Communication theory teaches us to tune out word imps as so much noise; psychotherapy warns us of madness.[17] But poetry, whatever else it is, is an attentiveness or attunement, an open-ness or receptiveness to the strangeness or otherness of words of just the sort that Cavell is describing here. One could as well say that poetry is a response to the uncanniness of ordinary language, where (again) what is uncanny is not simply the cor-poreality of language as such but the way in which this corpo-reality reorients our relation to language (not to say the world) by turning us into listeners rather than speakers. In poetry the corporeality of language addresses us.

With somewhat greater sublimity, and solemnity, Heidegger calls this phenomenon "having an experience *with* language," which is what occurs when "language brings itself to language."[18] It is what happens when language suddenly deprives us of subjective control, that is, when it takes us out of our role as speaking subjects and situates us outside itself in the position of respondents. Michael Davidson says: "I was faced by my own language staring me back in the face"; Cavell calls our attention to "words, leading lives of their own, staring back at us, calling upon one another, giving us away, alarming—because to note them is to see that they live in front of our eyes, within earshot, at every moment." As if my own language were not my possession but something outside my linguistic competence (as if the whole idea of linguistic competence were a subjectivist conceit). Imagine being face-to-face with language, language as exteriority, language that cannot be done away with by speaking or deciphering it: imagine this, and you are on the way to language, or to poetry.[19] Poetry is, let us say, a responsibility toward language, an unforgetting or acknowledgment—more or less in defiance of logic, linguistics, and philosophy of language—of the irreducibility of our speech to the status of an object, code, system, conceptual scheme, paradigm, prisonhouse, ideology, superstructure, or form of rule-governed, monological behavior.

Just so, in *Les mots et les choses* (1966) Michel Foucault goes so far to locate the origin of modern poetry as a response to the twofold effect of the Enlightenment to objectify language and to deploy it as an instrument of a subject-centered rationality that seeks to bring all that is, including language, under conceptual control: "at the beginning of the nineteenth century, at a time when language was burying itself within its own destiny as an object and allowing itself to be traversed, through and through, by knowledge, it was also reconstituting itself elsewhere, in an independent form, difficult of access, folded back upon the enigma of its own origin and existing wholly in reference to the pure act of writing." The term, "pure act of writing," derives from Maurice Blanchot's conception of *écriture* as an event in which literature comes into existence, not as the product of a writer's genius, imagination, consciousness, or mastery of language, but (on the contrary) as an interruption or reversal of consciousness that

turns subjectivity inside out, deprives it of rational control, exposes it to whatever is otherwise (the Outside, the Neutral, the
Unknown). As writing, Foucault says,

> literature becomes progressively more differentiated from
> a discourse of ideas, and encloses itself in a radical
> intransitivity; it becomes detached from all the values
> that were able to keep it in general circulation during
> the Classical age (taste, pleasure, naturalness, truth),
> and creatures within its own space everything that will
> ensure a ludic denial of them (the scandalous, the
> ugly, the impossible); it breaks with the whole defini-
> tion of *genres* as forms adapted to an order of repre-
> sentations, and becomes merely a manifestation of a
> language which has no other law than that of affirm-
> ing—in opposition to all other forms of discourse—its
> own precipitous existence.[20]

Literature in this sense (poetry made of words: the *es gibt* of
language) confronts the modern subject as a radical exteriority
that announces the limits of cognitive mastery. Poetry is language
that refuses to become an object; it is the withdrawal of language
from the world or, more accurately, from our grasp of the world
by means of concepts. Poetry is the original critique of the
subject, one might say the original critique of reason. Plato
understood as much.

Gadamer emphasizes this poetic critique when he speaks of
"the poetic work as a corrective for the ideal of objective determination and for the hubris of concepts" (GW8.237/PA190). In
particular, Gadamer has in mind the tendency of philosophical
language to become a fixed, technical vocabulary—a scholasticism. "The great Greek thinkers protected the fluidity of their
own language when they undertook to fix concepts in their
thematic analyses. But in opposition to this, there has always
been scholasticism—ancient, medieval, modern, contemporary. It
follows philosophy like a shadow, and it is almost possible to
determine the status of an attempt at thinking in terms of how
far it is able to break out of the petrification of handed down
philosophical language" (GW2.506/PA190). This is why philoso-

phy likewise needs a poetic or speculative experience with language—why it always needs poetry in its way as a "remembrance of language."

> The language of philosophizing was not made for phi-
> losophizing. Philosophy entangles itself in a constitu-
> tive language-need *[Sprachnot]*, and this language-need
> becomes all the more palpable the more the philoso-
> phizing person gets out in front of himself in his think-
> ing. In general it is the sign of the dilettante that
> concepts are arbitrarily constructed and enthusiastically
> 'defined.' The philosopher stirs up the observation
> powers of speech, and every stylistic boldness and act
> of violence has its place and succeeds in penetrating
> into the speech of those who would think-with and
> think-further *[mitdenken und weiterdenken]*. This means
> shaking up, extending, and throwing light on the ho-
> rizon of communication *[Verständigung]*. (GW2.507/
> PA191)[21]

Imagine philosophy as—quite as much as poetry—an event
at the limits of intelligibility!

The Aesthetics of Refusal

In his letter to Fred Dallmayr Gadamer says that "it is precisely
the new trajectories in thought opened up by the *later* Heidegger—
drawing into the hermeneutical dimension the themes of the
artwork, the thing, and language—that have guided my way, or
better confirmed my own path of thought" (DD94). What characterizes the artwork, the thing, and language is that each is
in its way self-secluding, ungraspable, resistant to conceptual
determination. In "Der Ursprung des Kuntswerkes" (1933–35),
Heidegger speaks of the way the thing resists our attempts to
turn it into an object. "The unpretentious thing evades thought
most stubbornly. Or can it be that this self-refusal *[Sichzurück-
halten]* of the mere thing, this self-contained independence,
belongs precisely to the nature of the thing. Must this strange

and uncommunicative feature *[Befremdende und Verschlossene]* of the nature of the thing become intimately familiar to thought that tries to think the thing? If so, then we should not force our way to its thingly character" (GA5.17/PLT32). This cautionary statement applies equally to the work of art and to language, which are thinglike in their "strange and uncommunicative" nature.

coming into the light of being

For Heidegger, the structure of the work of art is ontological rather than formal. This means first of all that the work of art is not an aesthetic object but an event that can be characterized phenomenologically in terms of disclosure or coming into the light of being: the *work* of the work of art is an opening up of the world to time and history (GW5.32/PLT45: "The work as work sets up a world. The work holds open the Open of the world"). But this opening of the world is not the whole story of the work of art. The work cannot be reduced to "phainaesthetics." The world is not brought into the open as such; rather, this event occurs within the limit or horizon of the earth, where the earth is that which remains undisclosed, outside the world and resistant to it. This resistance of the earth is as much the work of the work of art as is the disclosure of the world. "In setting up a world, the work sets forth the earth. . . . The work moves the earth itself into the Open of the world and keeps it there. *The work lets the earth be an earth*" (GA5.32/PLT46).

The earth is a figure of radical finitude, of pure exteriority, which Heidegger elucidates by way of the density or impermeability of a stone, which withdraws from our efforts to break it open and lay it bare. One might think of this refusal as the stone's testimony to the way the earth speaks. The earth, Heidegger says,

the EARTH

shows itself only when it remains undisclosed and unexplained *[unentborgen und unerklärt]*. Earth thus shatters every attempt to penetrate into it. It causes every merely calculating importunity upon it to turn into a destruction. This destruction may herald itself under the appearance of mastery and of progress in the form of the technical-scientific objectivation of nature, but this mastery nevertheless remains an impotence of the will. The earth appears openly cleared as itself only when it is perceived and preserved as that *the EXTERIORITY of EARTH puts into play the historicity of the world.*

which is by nature undisclosable *[Unerschliessbare], that which shrinks from every disclosure and constantly keeps itself closed up.* (GA5.33/PLT47)

NOT a FORM of Negation

But this closure is not formal. It is important not to think of the resistance of the earth as a form of negation or as if the earth were an autonomous entity sealed off in a region of aesthetic differentiation. Our ready-to-wear critical concepts conceal the way in which earth and world are exposed to one another. Heidegger thinks of their relation as a conflict or strife *(Streit)* that calls upon each to be what it is. It is a productive antagonism of mutual belonging rather than the more familiar dialectical struggle where opponents aim at overcoming and mastery of the other. The exteriority of the earth, for example, is what puts into play the historicity of the world. Think of the earth as anarchical in the etymological sense of being on the hither side of the world's principle of unity. Another way to put this would be to say that the alterity of the earth is its exteriority, its irreducibility to the world's concepts and categories. This after all is what the *materiality* of the work of art bears witness to. "The self-seclusion of earth . . . is not a uniform, inflexible staying under cover, but unfolds itself in an inexhaustible variety of simple modes and shapes." Heidegger singles out the sculptor, the painter, and the poet, each of whom works in what we call a particular medium, but the word "medium" is a misleading concept. The sculpting of the stone is not a use of it. Likewise the poem is made of language but is not a use of it. As if he had read Valéry, Heidegger says: "To be sure, the poet also uses the word—not, however, like ordinary speakers and writers who have to use them up, but rather in such a way that the word only now becomes and remains truly a word" (GA5.34/PLT47–48).

What is it for a word to be "truly a word"? Here one must imagine a word that is not exchangeable for something else: the word as pure exteriority. Likewise the work of art cannot serve as a substitute for whatever is not itself. It portrays nothing. As Heidegger likes to say, the work of art, before everything else, *is.* The fact that it is, is all that can be predicated of the work of art. This means that the work cannot be made a part of anything else. It is uncontainable within any totality.

the word as pure EXTERIORITY

The conflict or rift of world and earth constitutes the structure of the work of art and helps to explain the ontological exteriority of the work to the world. If the work works to hold open the Open of the world, the work itself withholds itself from this event and remains on the hither (an-archic) side of the world, as if it were excessive with respect to its own ontology, or as if there were no room in the world for works of art. To be sure, it seems at first as if the work of art—the Greek temple, for example—presides over the world as its centerpiece, the shrine around which everything is gathered into a unity. But the work is never part of the world's furniture; rather it holds in place the finitude of the world. Consider the fate of the work of art in view of the world's temporality. What happens to the work once the world is established? The temple after all is merely a ruin, a fragment from an incomplete time. It is, as Heidegger says of the work with respect to the world, self-standing, severed from all human ties, estranged from its surroundings. The work *is*. Its being is not a being-as but rather is non-identical in the manner of the *es gibt* or the *il y a*. "The more essentially the work opens itself, the more luminous becomes the uniqueness of the fact that it is rather than is not. The more essentially this thrust comes into the Open, the stranger *[befremdlicher]* and more solitary the work becomes" (GA5.53/PLT66).[22] This strangeness is not anthropological, that is, merely unfamiliar or exotic. The work is not otherworldly, existing in a domain of its own; it is non-worldly, not a being-in-the-world but earthly (dark and reserved: stone-like) in its createdness, excessive with respect to the world, but intimately, inescapably so. As such, it works as an intervention in the space of the world, exposing the world to what is not itself or to its outside. This intervention, this exposure to the outside, is the truth of the work, where truth is not correspondence or self-sameness but, strangely, untruth vis-à-vis the law of identity. In truth, the self-sameness of the world is interrupted (perhaps one could say: temporalized) by the work.[23] The work is a refusal of self-identity.[24] In "The Origin of the Work of Art," Heidegger characterizes this interruption or refusal of the same by the name of poetry *(Dichtung),* where "in the midst of what is, art breaks open an open place, in whose place everything is other than usual" (GA5.59/PLT72).[25]

the "OPEN PLACE"

Where is this "open place," where the non-identical comes into play? This, as it happens, is Paul Celan's question; it is the question of poetry.

A Poetics of Intimacy

"The objection is often made," Gadamer says in his essay "The Origin of the Work of Art," "that the basic concepts of Heidegger's later work cannot be verified" (GW3.258/HW105). But Gadamer thinks that, nevertheless, there is a deep internal kinship between Heidegger's thinking and modern poetry's radical thesis that "the work of art is language" (GW3.261/HW109). But it is only in Gadamer's work, and specifically in his encounter with Celan, that this kinship is brought to realization.

The thesis that the work of art is language leaves open the question of what language is. But on this question Gadamer has never hesitated to say: "Language . . . is always the language of conversation" ("Letter to Dallmayr," DD99). The importance of Paul Celan to Gadamer's thinking is that Celan's writings situate the radical thesis explicitly within the context of the main question of philosophical hermeneutics: What is it to be addressed? Language is not simply the medium of something that happens, of speech or dialogue or understanding; it is the event itself.

Gadamer

language is the event itself

Gadamer frequently refers to Celan's famous words from his Bremen speech in 1958:

CELAN's words

> Only one thing remained reachable, close and secure amid all losses: language. Yes, language. In spite of everything, it remained secure against loss. But it had to go through [hindurchgehen] its own lack of answers, through terrifying silence, through the thousand darknesses of murderous speech. It went through. It gave me no words for what was happening, but went through it. Went through and could resurface, 'enriched' ['angereichert'] by it all.
>
> In this language I tried, during those years and the years after, to write poems: in order to speak, to orient myself, to find out where I was, where I was going, to chart my reality.

It meant movement, you see, something happening, being *on the way* [*Ereignis, Bewegung, Unterwegs-sein*], an attempt to find a direction. Whenever I ask about the sense of it, I remind myself that this implies the question as to which sense is clockwise [*dass in dieser Frage auch die Frage nach dem Uhrzeigersinn mitspricht*].

For the poem does not stand outside time. True, it claims the infinite and tries to reach across time—but across, not above.

A poem, being an instance of language, hence essentially dialogue [*und damit seinem Wesen dia-logische ist*], may be a letter in a bottle thrown out to sea with the—surely not always strong—hope that it may somehow wash up somewhere, perhaps on a shoreline of the heart. In this way, too, poems are *on the way* [*unterwegs*]: they are headed toward.

Toward what? Toward something open, inhabitable, an approachable you [*auf ein ansprechbares Du*], perhaps, an approachable reality.

Such realities are, I think, at stake in the poem. I also believe that this kind of thinking accompanies not only my own efforts, but those of other, younger poets. Efforts of those who, with man-made stars flying overhead, unsheltered even by the traditional tent of the sky, exposed in an unsuspected, terrifying way, carry their existence into language, racked by reality and in search of it. (GW3.186/CP34–35)[26]

Poetry is, again, the unforgetting of language, in which we are reminded, first of all, that language is not a formal system; it is what philosophers call natural language—but perhaps one should use the older philological expression, *living* language: language whose mode of existence is the event, a language of *Erfahrung* that lives through or undergoes the experiences of all those who speak it and hear it, and which is therefore never self-identical but always on the way, *unterwegs*[27]—

what is it called, your country
behind the mountain, behind the year?
I know what it is called.
Like the winter's tale, it's called,
it's called the summer's tale,
your mother's threeyearland,
   that's what it was,
what it is,
it wanders everywhere, like
language. (PPC219)

wie heisst es, dein Land
hinterm Berg, hinterm Jahr?
Ich weiss, wie es heisst.
Wie das Wintermärchen, so heisst es,
es heisst wie das Sommermärchen,
das Dreijahreland deiner Mutter, das war es,
das ists,
es wandert überallhin, wie
die Sprache. (GW1.285)

Celan (Paul Antschel, later Ancel) was born into a German-speaking Jewish community in Bukovina, which was once part of the Austro-Hungarian empire, later was (and somewhat still is) part of Romania, then later was part of the Soviet Union, and now is (more or less) part of the Ukraine. What is it called, indeed! (Celan once referred to this region as "a victim of historylessness").[28] Not many maps bother to identify it. In 1941 the Jews of Bukovina were removed to concentration camps, where Celan's father died of typhus and where his mother was murdered. Celan survived the war in work camps. His first book of poems, written in German, was published in Vienna in 1947. Later he made his way to Paris, but he continued to write his poetry in German—but a non-identical German: a German outside of German.

a nomad language

Celan's German is "deterritorialized" in the sense in which Gilles Deleuze and Félix Guattari use this term in reference to Kafka, whose language was a German spoken in the Jewish community of Prague. Prague German is a language outside of language, a "nomad" language, where words leave behind the space of their meanings. Kafka's German is "reterritorialized" in Prague, where its sounds enter into a space that neutralizes their sense. Kafka intensifies the neutralization of German. He takes German into the space of Yiddish, where "he will make it cry with an extremely sober and rigorous cry. He will pull from it the barking of the dog, the cough of the ape, and the bustling of the beetle. He will turn syntax into a cry that will embrace the rigid syntax of this dried-up German. He will push it toward . . . an absolute deterritorialization, even if it is slow, sticky, coagulated. To bring language slowly and progressively to the desert. To use syntax in order to cry, to give a syntax to the cry."[29]

As in one of Celan's late poems:

ST
Ein Vau, pf, in der That,
schlägt, mps,
ein Sieben-Rad:

o
oo
ooo
O (GW3.136)

Imagine this O as the basic unit of Celan's poetry.

Celan's work gives special meaning to the corporeality and exteriority of poetic language; it brings these limit-concepts together in a unique way. In "Der Meridian," his famous speech on the occasion of receiving the Büchner prize in 1960, Celan asks whether there is any sense to the question, What is art?—which is a question that is raised in Büchner's writings, where art is figured in terms of puppets, monkeys or the monkey-shape (*Affengestalt:* gorilla-suit?), automatons, and Medusa heads (GW3.187–88/CP37–38).

"It is easy to talk about art," says Celan. "But when there is talk of art, there is often somebody who does not really

[handwritten: Someone who hears, But does not understand]

listen"—that is, someone who hears but who doesn't understand.
This is not an altogether bad thing. Imagine "someone who
hears, listens, looks ... and then does not know what it was
about. But who hears the speaker, 'sees him speaking,' who
perceives language as a physical shape, and also ... breath, that
is, direction and destiny [*Der aber den Sprechenden hört, der ihn
'sprechen sieht,' der Sprache wahrgenommen hat und Gestalt und
zugleich ... auch Atem, das heisst, Richtung und Schicksal]*"
(GW3.188/CP39). Someone who cannot see through things, who
remains on this side, on the skin or fleshly side, of discourse,
where language is still visible, or (more intimately) where it can
be felt as a breath, where it is an event occurring just now, just
this one time, to you.[30]

Celan's reference in this context is to a character in Büchner's
Dantons Tod, Lucile, "who is artblind [*Kunstblinde],* for whom
language is tangible and like a person [*für die Sprache etwas
Personhaftes und Wahrnehmbares hat]*" (GW3.189/CP40). At the
end of *Dantons Tod,* Lucile, at the guillotine, cries out (absurdly),
"Long live the King." Celan calls this a *Gegenwort:* "It is an act
of freedom. It is a step" (GW3.189/CP40).

Celan wants to give this *Gegenwort* the name of poetry: the
discourse of the *Kunstblinde* who perceive language as something on the hither, exterior, fleshly side of the world of the
spirit. But "discourse" is not the right word, or at all events not
Celan's word. Celan is explicit that poetry is non-aesthetic, that
is, it is not a work or process of art. Its mode of being is not
that of the *oeuvre* but of *désoeuvrement,* worklessness.[31] Its movement is not toward a point of being finished but a ceaseless,
open-ended movement of indeterminacy toward what is always
elsewhere, a pure exteriority. Imagine poetry as a name of this
elsewhere. Not a movement of the true but of freedom.

[handwritten margin: PURE EXTERIORITY]

In Celan's text the relationship between poetry and art is
marked out in part by two characters in Büchner's writings:
Lucille, the *Kunstblinde,* and Lenz, the artist, a self-forgetting *I,*
one "whose eyes and mind are occupied with art" (GW3.193/
CP44). Lenz, who says that "One would like to be a Medusa's
head" in order to grasp what is natural, not so much to make
it unnatural as to situate it differently as something fixed and
self-identical, possessing objectivity and value—but therefore

[handwritten: the Poem simply stops for a moment]

something no longer human, since what is human cannot be fixed or objectified without cost.[32] Art perhaps pays the price by "going [Celan says] beyond what is human, stepping into the realm which is turned toward the human, but *uncanny*—the realm where the monkey, the automatons and with them . . . oh, art, too, seem to be at home *[Das ist ein Hinaustreten aus dem Menschlichen, ein Sichhinausbegeben in einem dem Menschlichen zugewandten und unheimlichen Bereich—denselben, in dem die Affengestalt, die Automaten und damit . . . ach, auch die Kunst zuhause zu sein scheinen]*" (GW3.192/CP42–43).

Art is estrangement, self-estrangement (causing self-forgetfulness) but also estrangement from the human. Art is incapable of intimacy. Art is uncanny in the sense of monstrous, the not quite or no longer human, the almost- or once-human. Poetry is different from this, from art, but not in the way the familiar is different from the strange or the human from the almost-human. Poetry is also uncanny, but differently so, with another sort of strangeness (GW3.195/CP47): not uncanny in the way of art but in the way things are strange when they are no longer subject to our concepts and categories, when they escape us. Imagine things freeing themselves from the meaningful, becoming, not meaningless, but anarchic and non-identical.

This is how it is with poetry in Celan's text, where the poem is never in place or in view as something self-identical but always something *unterwegs:* on the way, that is, not becoming or in process as if moving toward repose or definition or the objectivity of the aesthetic work but nomadic, traversing meridians, encountering space as a radical exteriority outside the categories of inside and outside. In his Bremen address Celan spoke of poetry (or of the poem) explicitly in Heidegger's vocabulary: *Ereignis, Bewegung, Unterwegssein* (GW3.186/CP34). These are the terms in which Heidegger tries to clarify the question of thinking. Thinking for Heidegger is not a species of reasoning; it is not a conceptual movement or movement of systematic construction. It is an event of language that is irreducible to the propositional style of philosophical discourse. So, like poetry, thinking can and needs to be situated outside of discourse. In *Was heisst Denken?* Heidegger emphasizes that thinking is responsive rather than assertive, paratactic (and therefore fragmen-

thinking — always on the way

An Introduction to Gadamer's Poetics 21

tary) rather than syntactic and unifying, wayward rather than progressive—incessantly wayward, always on the way, restless even in the moment of pausing, always called out (as if by poetry?) into a place where everything is otherwise.

The poem for Celan belongs to this ontological condition of *Unterwegssein:* always on the way. "Perhaps—I am only speculating," Celan says, "—perhaps poetry, like art, moves with the oblivious self into the uncanny and strange to free itself again. Though where? In which place? how? as what? *[vielleicht geht die Dichtung, wie die Kunst, mit einem selbstvergessenen Ich zu jenem Unheimlichen und Fremden, und setz sich—doch wo? doch an welchem Ort? doch womit? doch als was?—wieder frei?]*" (GW3.193/ CP44). Open questions: how to keep them open?

Clearly *Unterwegssein* is not a discursive or productive movement of *poiesis.* Poetry is on the hither side of discourse and art, the side of corporeality and exteriority, as when Celan says: I believe that I have met poetry in the figure of Lucile, and Lucile perceives language as shape, direction, breath *[nimmt Sprache als Gestalt und Richtung und Atem wahr].*" To which Celan adds: "I am looking for the same thing here, in Büchner's work. I am looking for Lenz himself, as a person [i.e., not as a character in a text but as himself, walking through the mountains on the 20th of January], I am looking for his shape: for the sake of the place of poetry, for the sake of liberation, for the sake of the step *[als Person, ich suche seine Gestalt: um des Ortes der Dichtung, um der Freisetzung, um des Schrittes willen]*" (GW3.194/CP45).

Atem, Ort, Freisetzung (releasement), *Schritt:* an odd vocabulary for a poetics.

Perhaps the most famous line in "Der Meridian" is: *"Dichtung: das kann eine Atemwende bedeuten"* (GA3.195/CP47).[33] A turning of the breath (if that is what *Atemwende* is) can answer to the name of poetry; or, perhaps, vice versa: this event, this breath, is what poetry responds to. Poetry is perhaps this response or responsiveness, this responsibility for the side of speech that resists reduction or the turning of a breath into a mediation or expression. Possibly the poem is as much the taking of a breath as the expulsion of it ("A breath for nothing," says Rilke, breathing freely, without constriction, not having to speak); or perhaps, as in Levinas's account of *le dehors* in *Autrement qu'être,*

freedom is breath, "the breathing of outside air, where inward-
ness frees itself from itself, and is exposed to all the winds."[34]
Here breathing is non-subjective: it means taking in the air that
belongs to "an outside where nothing covers anything, non-
protection, the reverse of a retreat, homelessness, non-world,
non-inhabitation, layout without security" (AE275–76/OTB179).
As if there were a link between breath and exile.

Celan perhaps gives us a glimpse of this "outside" in
"Gespräch im Gebirg" (1959), where two Jews (called "wind-
bags" [Geschwätzigen]) encounter one another on alien ground.
Levinas himself remains deeply suspicious of this region, which
he associates with the il y a and what he takes to be Heidegger's
dehumanized ontology. To the openness of the Open, the open
place where everything is strange or non-identical, he opposes
the openness of the face, whose breath is "the wind of alterity":

> In human breathing, in its everyday equality, perhaps
> we have to already hear the breathlessness of an inspi-
> ration that paralyzes essence [i.e., self-identity], that
> transpierces it with an inspiration by the other, an
> inspiration that is already expiration, that "rends the
> soul"! It is the longest breath there is, spirit. Is man not
> the living being capable of the longest breath in inspi-
> ration, without a stopping point, and in expiration, not
> to thought.[37]

But the poem is also an event of language (Ereignis), as in
modernity's radical thesis:

> The poem speaks. It is mindful of its dates, but it
> speaks. True, it speaks only on its own, its very own
> behalf [immer nur in seiner eigenen, allereigensten
> Sache].
>   But I think—and this will hardly surprise you—
> that the poem has always hoped, for this very reason,
> to speak also on behalf of the strange [auch in
> fremder]—no, I can no longer use this word here—on
> behalf of the other, who knows, perhaps of an alto-
> gether other [gerade auf diese Weise in eines Anderen

Sache zu sprechen—wer weiss, vielleicht in eines ganz Anderen *Sache].* (GW3.196/CP48)

Poetry speaks not as a medium but on its own, self-standing and reserved—the way a person speaks. At the same time, and perhaps precisely because of its withdrawal from the language of mediation, it speaks for another, or perhaps for the other of all others (*eines ganz Anderen Sache),* an otherness more Blanchovian than Levinasian, not just that which is otherwise than being, the ethical, but that which is neither one nor the other, outside even the ethical relation in which an I is turned inside out before the *Autrui.*

A pure exteriority: a freedom for which we have no words. In modern tradition freedom is Kantian: it is the free subject, the self-regulating, self-same ego over and against which nothing is free but is rather subject or subjected to cognition and the laws of identity. For Celan, as for Maurice Blanchot, freedom is the outside, the region of the other, of others near and far, of foreignness itself. The movement of poetry is toward this region, or toward "the 'otherness' which it can reach and be free *[auf jenes 'Anderes' zu, das es sich als erreichbar, als freizusetzen],* which is perhaps vacant and at the same time turned like Lucile, let us say, turned toward it, toward the poem" (GW3.197/CP48).

"Movement," however, is a questionable term. Celan's text is not a narrative of a journey or a quest; the poem is not an alter ego but an event of releasement—one could do worse than borrow Heidegger's word, *Gelassenheit,* letting-be or letting-go, which is not a performative that an agent might or might not take up but a condition of openness toward what is outside and uncontainable within our discursive fields. Heidegger calls it *die Offenheit für das Geheimnis,* where *das Geheimnis* is usually translated as "mystery," but which is perhaps better understood topologically as that which is set apart, elsewhere, outside, not what we have made our own but that which is self-standing and alone like the thing.[38] For Heidegger *Gelassenheit* is not a cognitive movement of thinking but the ethical responsiveness of thinking to what withdraws from the world, a responsiveness that is no less ethical for being a *Gelassenheit zu den Dingen:* a releasement turned toward things and not just toward other people.[39]

At all events, when Celan speaks (strangely) of the self-assertion of the poem—*Das Gedicht behauptet sich* (GW3.197/CP49: Rosemarie Waldrop translates this as "The poem holds its ground")—this event is as much a movement of displacement as of definition. The text reads like a parody of definition or the positioning of an object: "the poem asserts itself on its own margin *[das Gedicht behauptet sich am Rande seiner selbst]*." Imagine the place of poetry as something other than a position to be occupied.[40] Celan in fact deliberately mixes his metaphors, displacing space into time (and back again), in order to confound any thought of fixing poetry in its place: "*es ruft und holt sich, um bestehen zu können, unausgesetzt aus seinem Schon-nicht-mehr in sein Immer-noch zurück*" (GW3.197/CP49: the poem, as Waldrop translates, "calls and pulls itself back . . . from an 'already-no-more' into a 'still-here' "). Put it that the poem's presence is not a self-presence; it never coincides with itself in a moment of self-identity. *Immer-noch* is not a point in which something asserts itself as such; it is rather like the point where the thing, in Heidegger's formulation, stands on its own, alone in its "self-containment" (*Insichruhen*: as if reposing in itself ["Der Ursprung des Kunstwerkes," GA5.11/PLT26]). The poem is singular, not objective but thinglike insofar as it is outside the alternatives of subject and object; or, in other words, free.

A poetics of non-identity is in Celan's language a poetics of *Entsprechung* (GW3.197/CP49), where *Entsprechung* is something like a condition of attunement in which one is turned toward the other in an event of listening. *Entsprechung* describes very well Lucile's response to language as the breath and flesh of what is singular or external to the space that discourse otherwise opens up for our habitation, namely the world of talk and action where things are taken up in the movement of concepts or taken in hand through clarification and description. The poem frees language from this logical domain. It is, in Celan's words, "language actualized, set free under the sign of a radical individuation which, however, remains as aware of the limits drawn by language as of the possibilities it opens *[Sondern aktualisierte Sprache, freigesetzt unter dem Zeichen einer zwar radikalen, aber gleichzeitig auch der ihr von der Sprache gezogenen Grenzen, der ihr von der Sprache erschlossenen Möglichkeiten eingedenk bleibenden Individuation]*" (GW3.197/CP49).

"Individuation" is not a term of identity, of naming or nameability; it does not belong to the relation of sameness and difference. Think of it rather as a term of intimacy. Celan clarifies it in terms of what names cannot reach: the *Dasein* and *Kreatürlichkeit* of the poet. The poem actualizes language, but not as if it were a system; actualizing means situating—a movement away from rules and universals. The poem brings language down to earth, situates it in a here and now specific to the *Dasein* and *Kreatürlichkeit* of the one who speaks (but also, it turns out, of the other who listens as well). *Dasein* and *Kreatürlichkeit* are not features or attributes (Heidegger would say, they are ontological rather than ontic); Celan calls them *Neigungswinkels,* which is a word made up of nods and winks, irreproducible shapes or turns that belong to the poem as an irreducible event of language (what Lucile perceives: how she reads). Think of *der Neigungswinkel* as a path which a poem opens up to us. The poem is not a species of ostensive discourse: it does not point, rather it inclines, perhaps with a subtlety not easy to register.

Whereto? Inclines whereto?

Celan's language is full of Heideggerian nods and winks: "The poem is solitary. It is solitary and on the way *[Das Gedicht ist einsam. Es ist einsam und unterwegs]*" (GW3.198/CP49). Nomadic, deterritorialized: always elsewhere, always exterior. This elsewhere is perhaps already marked by the poem as the hint that it attends to, cares for and follows; it is the other in the poem, not so much a formal or distinctive feature as a fact of its irreducibility to the objective condition of work or text, as if it could be constituted by what it is not. "The poem," Celan says, "intends another, needs this other, needs an opposite. It goes toward it, bespeaks it *[Das Gedicht will zu einem Andern, es braucht dieses Andere, es braucht ein Gegenüber. Es sucht es auf, es spricht sich ihm zu]*" (GW3.198/CP49).

It is difficult to clarify this other, because it is an alterity in excess of strangeness: beyond the other there is *eines ganz Anderen Sache* that Celan's readers sometimes want to divinize, but which is perhaps no more than the region of the non-identical, of open indeterminacy, that the poem opens up with the strangeness of its language. Certainly it is correct to think of the poem in terms of an ethical relation. It is an instance of attentiveness, as if to another human being. *Entsprechung*, after all, does not mean agreement in the sense of *adequatio*; it is a term of responsibility, of listening rather than seeing. It is a dialogical rather than a logical concept. Its attentiveness is not scrutiny, mere attention to details, but an attentiveness of the ear and of memory. So not surprisingly Celan figures the poem as a conversation, where attentiveness is a condition of possibility. It is this possibility that speaks to Gadamer. Should this be allegorized as ethics? Or as ontology?

Levinas appropriates Celan to his conception of ethical alterity, explicitly contra Heidegger's ontology, in "Paul Celan: De l'être à l'autre."[41] Philippe Lacoue-Labarthe argues to the contrary that Celan cannot be separated out from Heidegger so easily. There is, he says, no other that is "otherwise than being." "Poetry's 'you-saying,' its naming, is a way of 'Being-saying.' "[42] The interest of Gadamer's poetics is the way it helps us to understand the reductions in each of these appropriations. On the one hand, for Levinas there can never be an ethical relation with poetry, because there is always more to a poem than the ethical relation. As Blanchot suggested many years ago, Levinas "mistrusts poetry and poetic activity" because it is made of language.[43] As such it is (among other things) what must be overcome if there is to be ethics as first philosophy. For Levinas, there can be no question of allowing oneself to be addressed by a poem. This is very odd, but perhaps no more so than Lacoue-Labarthe's attempt to idealize the poem, to disembody it as "an act of thought"—"the thought of the presence of the present, or of the other of that which is present: the thought of no-thingness *[pensée du né-ant]* (of being), that is to say, the thought of time."[44] But this is once more to reduce the corporeality of the poem; it is to allegorize the poem by subsuming it within the monologue of philosophy: "The experience of the you, the encounter, opens onto nothing other than the experience of being" (p. 98).

Gadamer's perspective requires neither ethics nor ontology. The poem is something that addresses us, that intercepts us, on whatever way we are, and situates us in a space of open indeterminacy where the rule of identity and the legislation of concepts are no longer in control. As Gadamer says (more or less repeatedly), the importance of the question, "Wer bin ich und wer bist du?," is that it always remains open, and that this openness is renewed from poem to poem, "where 'I,' 'you' and 'we' are pronounced in an utterly direct, shadowy-uncertain and constantly changing way *[wo ganz unvermittelt, schattenhaft-unbestimmt und in beständig wechselnder Weise "ich", "du", "wir", gesagt]*" (GW9.384–85). Gadamer's commentary is a close study of the multiple changes that Celan rings on the "I" and the "you." But what matters for Gadamer is not the identity of the "I" or the "you" but the intimacy between them—an intimacy which is outside the determinacy of meaning, or which is not an intimacy of knowing and being known but an intimacy mediated by strangeness (GW9.399–400). This intimacy—*Alleinsein in wechselseitiger Vertrautheit*, Gadamer calls it (GW9.400)—is perhaps the main theme of Gadamer's commentary on Celan.

Here Gadamer is in tune with Ossip Mandelstam's essay, "The Interlocutor," which was translated into French for the first time in 1959 on Celan's instigation and which seems to have shaped Celan's poetics in a decisive way. Mandelstam stresses the dialogical character of poetry, which is always in the vocative case, but it is a dialogue structured by the distance and foreignness that separates the poem and its other. Mandelstam says: "poetry as a whole is always directed toward a more or less distant, unknown addressee."[45] This distance, this strangeness, is not an obstacle to be overcome but rather something the poem makes room for and, so to speak, invites. Think of the poem as leaving a place within itself, a free space, for this unknown "you" (who might be anyone, no matter how strange or foreign). This seems exactly Celan's point: "Only the space of this conversation can establish what is addressed, can gather it into a 'you' around the naming and speaking I. But this 'you,' come about by dint of being named and addressed, brings its otherness into the present [i.e., into the poem]. Even in the here and now of the poem—and the poem has only this one, unique, momentary present—even in this immediacy and nearness, the otherness gives voice to what is most its own: its time" (GW3.198/CP50). If the poem actualizes language in terms of the nearness (or *hereness)* and creatureliness of the one who speaks, it also actualizes it for (and with) the other—the stranger who is addressed, whose own time is now also, strange as it may seem, internal to the diurnal course or waywardness of the poem. Actualization is an event of intimacy without identity and perhaps even without the communication of meaning or the agreement of subjects. It is not an intersubjective intimacy but, as Gadamer says, an intimacy characterized by "the remoteness of the one nearest to us [die Ferne des Allernächsten]" (GW9.400).

Aktualität

Celan speaks of "actualizing language [aktualisierte Sprache]" (GW3.197), that is, bringing it into the here and now. *Aktualisierten* (or, sometimes, *Vergegenwärtigung*) is a term of art in hermeneutics, where it has a complex or multi-directional application. For Gadamer it is an event that occurs when a text speaks to me— an event that is irreducible to the deciphering of meaning, since it very often takes the form of being brought up short by a text that does not answer my expectations of meaning and perhaps does not even respond to my interrogations, my research and analysis, concerning what it says. Rather, the movement of questioning is toward me, and all my familiar concepts—my whole way of making sense of things—might go to pieces in the event. For Gadamer this is a hermeneutical experience in a way that my encounter with a text that simply confirms my sense of how things are is not. For whatever happens, a text that intercepts me and interrupts my self-understanding now becomes part of or, indeed, actualizes my definition of reality as that which cannot be done away with. Reality of course is what we know, but our knowing consists in being exposed to the world or to history rather than in conceptual command of it. Being exposed is arguably the hermeneutical medium of historical consciousness, as Gadamer's analysis of *das wirkungsgeschichtliche Bewusstein* shows (WM322–39/TM352–56).[46] At all events to be interrupted by a text is always a moment of critique, but it is more, because the text now has a claim on me that I may never be able to settle. Suddenly I find myself defined by this claim, as if it now mirrored a part of me that I may hardly know how to recognize, but which I cannot renounce. The text exposes me to myself (GW8.102/RB11).

Say that I am part of the text's present, but only as an outsider. Gadamer always emphasizes that he reads Celan from in front of the text, not as someone privy to its secrets.[47] He thus

Szondi's method of

Pöggeler

differentiates himself both from Peter Szondi's method, which is to gloss the poem's references and allusions from an insider's point of view, speaking with the authority of friendship and as if in the poet's place; and from Otto Pöggeler's method of research that distances the poem by recontextualizing it within the historical and cultural background of Jewish mystical traditions. Both methods objectify the text in a way that excludes in principle the sense of intimacy that characterizes Gadamer's experience of the "I" and the "you." Derrida echoes Gadamer when he says that Celan's poetry outlives its witnesses and its shibboleths. "The poem speaks," Derrida says, "even should none of its references be intelligible, none other than the Other, the one to whom it addresses itself and to whom it speaks in saying that it speaks to him. Even if it does not reach and leave its mark, at least it calls to, the Other. Address takes place."[48] One cannot respond to this address by supplying it with special information.

Gadamer speaks of an intimacy mediated by strangeness, but intimacy still. Actualization is not only a critical event that turns me inside out in front of the text. It is an event of appropriation in which I make the thing my own even though I remain a stranger to it, knowing only what I know and not what the poet knew or what can be determined by specialists. The text, after all, speaks to my situation and not to me as a disengaged subject. I cannot reflect myself out of my situation: I cannot engage the text from outside my own skin. My relation to the text is outside the subject-object relation of spectatorship and cognition. It is a relation of non-expertise. It is a relation that Gadamer sometimes characterizes with the phrase, "aesthetic nondifferentiation," where the work of art is no longer an object for me but is rather an event of self-presentation that catches me up in its open-ended activity or *energeia*.   ENERGEIA

In "Phänomenologischer und semantischer Zugang zu Celan?" Gadamer speaks of reading as a "completion" of the poem. And he thinks of himself as seeking the "unity of meaning" in each poem. Obviously, neither of these statements makes sense from the standpoint of traditional aesthetics which sees the work of art as an autonomous and autotelic entity, a finished object even when, as in the case of Celan's poetry, the work is formally and analytically a fragment. But Gadamer understands the work of art first of all in its temporality. This means not only that the work exists in time as a historical document; it also means that it is temporal in its very nature, which is to say that despite its formal character as a finished piece of work it is at the same time structured as an event, as something "at work" or "in play" and therefore also unfinished. Of course we can position ourselves outside the temporality of the work by adopting the attitude of disinterested analysis. We can hold to the principle of aesthetic distance that frames the work of art in a timeless domain of the spirit. We can always gloss each and every detail of the work from countless scholarly and critical perspectives. But in so doing we close ourselves off to the work. It cannot speak to us; we have, in so many words, censored it. We miss the way the work draws time—its own as well as ours—into its play. For Gadamer, understanding is never an exercise of knowingness.

Gadamer's analysis of play in *Truth and Method* is well known. As an addendum to his discussion Gadamer speaks of the "occasionality" of the work of art—as in *Hamlet,* for example, where the historical and political context of the play is "at play" in the work, not as so many allusions that research might quantify, but (on the contrary) as that which remains unspoken—part of the aura of the work or resonance that remains for the audience or reader to register. This is part of the claim that the work has on us. As Gadamer says—and this is perhaps his most important statement of hermeneutical *praxis:*

> it is part of the reality of a play that it leaves an indefinite space around its real theme. A play in which everything is completely motivated creaks like a machine. It would be a false reality if the action could all be calculated out like an equation. Rather, it becomes a play of reality when it does not tell the spectator everything, but only a little more than he customarily understands in his daily round. The more that remains open, the more freely does the process of understanding succeed—i.e., the process of transposing what is shown in the play to one's own world and, of course, also to the world of one's own political experience. (WM471/TM498)[49]

It is this notion of the temporality of the work—the work as event and as play rather than as an aesthetic appearance—that Gadamer returns to in his attempt to come to terms with the radical thesis of aesthetic modernity. The major theoretical text in this case is "Die Aktualität des Schönen. Kunst als Spiel, Symbol, and Fest" (1974). The radical difference between the classical and the modern avant-garde can be mediated by thinking of the work in both instances as an intransitive movement, a being-in-play that is "not tied down to any goal" (GW8.113/RB22)—recall Celan's recourse to this concept in his characterization of the poem as a movement, a being "on the way." Following Aristotle, Gadamer calls it a "self-movement [*Selbstbewegung*]": "play appears as a self-movement that does not pursue any particular end or purpose so much as movement *as* movement, exhibiting so to speak a phenomenon of excess, of living self-representation [*der Selbstdarstellung des Lebendigseins*]" (GW8.114/RB23).

Now the crucial point is obviously that this play is not a sealed-off event that occurs in isolation. On the contrary, "the act of playing always requires a 'playing along with [*Mitspielen*]'" (GW8.114/RB23). Gadamer's idea is that modern art in particular calls for *Mitspielen*. "One of the basic impulses of modern art has been the desire to break down the distance separating the audience, the 'consumers,' and the public from the work of art." Gadamer mentions Brecht, "who specifically fought against our being absorbed in a theatrical dream-world as a feeble substitute for human and social consciousness of solidarity. He deliberately destroyed scenic realism, the normal expected of a play. But this desire to transform the distance of the onlooker into the involvement of the participant can be discerned in every form of modern experimentation in the arts" (GW8.115/RB24).

But if the formal unity and, let us say, the semantic and aesthetic identity of the work is destroyed, the "hermeneutic identity" of the work remains unaffected. What is this "hermeneutic identity"? Gadamer writes:

The concept of the work is in no way tied to a classical ideal of harmony. Even if the forms in which

some positive identification is made are quite different,
we still have to ask how it actually comes about that
the work addresses us. But there is yet another aspect
here. If the identity of the work is as we have said,
then the genuine reception and experience of the work
of art can exist only for one who "plays along [mitspielt],"
that is, one who performs in an active way himself.
Now how does that actually happen? Certainly not
simply through retention of something in memory. In
that case there would still be identification, but without
that particular assent by virtue of which the work means
something to us. What gives the work its identity as
work? What makes this what we call a hermeneutic
identity? Obviously, this further formulation means that
its identity consists precisely in there being something
to "understand," that it asks to be understood in what
it "says" or "intends." The work issues a challenge
which expects to be met. It requires an answer—an
answer that can only be given by someone who has
accepted the challenge. And that answer must be his
own, and given actively. The participant belongs to the
play. (GW8.116/RB25-26)

The "hermeneutic identity" of the work cannot be separated from
the event in which we are addressed—and here "address has to
be understood in the strong sense of being interrupted, that is,
of being taken out of our usual mode of self-possession and
caught up in the working or, as the case may be, the "unworking"
of the work.

    Gadamer mentions a bottle-rack exhibited as a work of art.
The idea here is not simply to gaze at the bottle-rack as hard as
one can in order to "see" it as a work of art, because, after all,
the thing is just what it appears to be: a bottle-rack. The point
is that there is a context here, an aesthetic event (which perhaps
includes the artist's attempt to explode the whole idea of the
work of art as a quasi-transcendental object) that we need to get
into and understand as if from the inside out, that is, as a
participant in the event. Gadamer and Arthur Danto are close
here. In a famous essay, "The Artworld," Danto says that every-

Danto — (handwritten)

thing depends on how we situate ourselves within art history—how one inhabits the artworld in which the event takes place.

Danto's example is Andy Warhol's Brillo box, which is a work of art that, empirically, can hardly be distinguished from an ordinary Brillo box.

> What in the end makes the difference between a Brillo box and a work of art consisting of a Brillo box is a certain theory of art. It is the theory that takes it up into the world of art, and keeps it from collapsing into the real object which it is (in a sense of *is* other than that of artistic identification). Of course, without the theory, one is unlikely to see it as art, and in order to see it as part of the artworld, one must have mastered a good deal of artistic theory as well as a considerable amount of the history of recent New York painting. It could not have been art fifty years ago. But then there could not have been, everything being equal, flight insurance in the Middle Ages, or Etruscan typewriter erasers. The world has to be ready for such things, the artworld no less than the real one. It is the role of artistic theories, these days as always, to make the artworld, and art, possible. It would, I should think, never have occurred to the painters of Lascaux that they were producing *art* on those walls. Not unless they were neolithic aestheticians.[50]

(handwritten margin: is it the ? not then. First —)

What Gadamer calls the "hermeneutic identity" of the artwork would be the sense it makes within the historical situation in which it appears. The point is that the work can address us only if we are ourselves part of this situation and can enter into the event in which the artwork makes its appearance and understand its relevance to the situation—its *aktualität*. Understanding the artwork means understanding its *aktualität*, that is, understanding the situation in light of the work's appearance and the work in light of the situation. But this is also in some sense a self-understanding since we ourselves belong to this situation: we are ourselves actualized by the work's appearance. *"Der Mitspieler gehört zum Spiel"* (GW8.117).

the resistance of a work

Tenebra

"Every work leaves the person who responds to it a certain leeway, a space *[Spielraum]* to be filled in by himself" (GW8.117/ RB26). Obviously this is not an unproblematical concept, for (as Gadamer himself insists) there always remains the sense in which the work of art is self-standing and reserved. Part of its play is its refusal to be played willy-nilly. Gadamer's aesthetics is always an "aesthetics of refusal" in the sense in which we have used this term. The resistance of the work to our appropriation of it will always remain part of our hermeneutical experience. There will always be a difference between the work and my understanding of it. This comes out dramatically in Gadamer's reading of many of Celan's poems—most notably, "Tenebrae"—which he takes as only a Christian reader could, but which a Jewish reader, as John Felstiner has shown, will always interpret differently.[51] But, again, this difference—this conflict of interpretations—is testimony to the temporality of art and poetry. "A universal thought dispenses with communication," says Levinas, but this can never be true of a discourse in which I am addressed by another.[52] What this means, however, is that the "I" and the "you" are not simply categories deployed impersonally across grammatical space. As Gadamer says, the "I" of the poem appropriates me, situates me in its time and space, but not as someone else whom I am to impersonate; on the contrary, the poem forces me to confront myself in its time.

Hence the cognitive dissonance that Gadamer himself registers when, reading "In die Rillen," he encounters Celan's terrible "theology of a self-withholding heaven *[verweigernden Himmels]*" (GW9.392). "All that we have from this self-withholding heaven," Gadamer says, "is the word. Is that what is meant? Something so Lutheran?" Hardly. "These are bitter lines," Gadamer says. The word that is given offers nothing of Christian comfort. However one takes it, "it is clear that nothing can be disclosed about heaven except what you—once again this unknown You—force through the porousness of the obstructing door. This is not a flowing message of salvation" (GW9.393). The "theology of the *Deus absconditus*" is the theology of the Holocaust, which is the event above all others in which Jews experienced their absolute abandonment; and not Jews only. The poem exposes even the Christian reader to its time in which the absence of the sacred is "shattering" (GW9.394). Shattering, not so much because, as Geoffrey Hartman says, the Holocaust "challenges the credibility of redemptive thinking," as because it deprives Christianity of the history to which it thought it would always belong.[53] Imagine salvation not as a message but as a history that perhaps somewhere continues on its way but to which Christianity can no longer lay any claim. So we may think of Celan's poetry as, among other things, a *Gegenwort* that exposes Christianity to its historicity, or (more severely) to the fact that history is not something that a theology can ever make intelligible or even bear to confront. Celan's thought might be: poetry, but no theology, after Auschwitz. And of course this thought applies to a good deal more than theology.

At all events Gadamer shows that the question of what must the reader know in order to understand Celan's poetry is the wrong one to ask (GW9.443). Gadamer has always regarded texts from something like a Lutheran point of view, where the idea is that the Bible is not a book of secrets but a self-interpreting text that addresses everyone. The task of reading is to allow what is familiar in the text to illuminate what is strange or obscure. This is Gadamer's approach to Celan. In principle there is no one whom the poem excludes from its audience. Gadamer's motto might be: No more shibboleths—for it seems to be part of the hermeneutical claim to universality that no one is without interpretive resources:

> What one person knows from experience, another knows only from books. One person knows about, say, the German-Slavic East, Jewish ritual, or even Kabbalistic mysticism; another finds orientation only by using a lexicon, or through arduous reading. This is also true of associative reference *[gegenwörtlicher Bezug]* to what has been said before. One person hears George and Rilke, as perhaps the poet did, or even French language and poetry, again perhaps as the poet did; another does not. One person knows from his or her own language usage a technical expression used by the poet; another can only become familiar with it slowly. Such specialities are constantly in play. (GW9.433)

But Gadamer's real point is that the hermeneutical question of what it is to be addressed cannot be clarified in terms of exegesis and decipherment. The poem does not address us as cognitive subjects seeking conceptual clarification and control—on the contrary, it seems to be in the nature of poetry to take us out of the relation of knowing. Again, Plato knew as much. Meanwhile the moral for Gadamer is that the priority of being over consciousness is axiomatic and has its most important application in just this context of how we stand with respect to texts that matter to us, for what these texts address is not how much we know but precisely how we stand. Gadamer's claim— "I believe that I have more or less understood these poems" (GW9.428)—is not a claim to knowledge but just a claim that they speak to him, and it entails the understanding and acknowledgment that the world of these poems is one to which he is very much a stranger. So the question is perhaps why they matter to him.

The answer to this question is partly theoretical in the sense which I have tried to clarify, namely that it is precisely one's strangeness before a text that is characteristic of the hermeneutical situation par excellence. The challenge of modern art and poetry is not to reduce the work of art to transparency but to understand how it is with us with respect to the history in which a text by Gertrude Stein or the music of John Cage give the definition of reality. This is the challenge that Gadamer takes up—rather heroically, when one thinks of it, since he does so at the end of an already illustrious career as a Plato scholar and as the foundational figure of philosophical hermeneutics. There is also the answer that Gadamer belongs to the tradition of German idealism in which the reading of poetry is still a philosophical task. The tradition, and the practice, will perhaps die with him. The question of why poetry should matter to philosophy at all has perhaps already been lost to reflection. Maybe all we can say now is that the poems of Paul Celan cannot be evaded. They belong not just to the history of art or the history of modernity; they are interventions in the existence of our time, and this is how Gadamer responds to them.

Notes to Bruns's Introduction

1. See "Der 'eminent' Text und seine Wahrheit" (1986). The eminent text is one that cannot be done away with by means of interpretation. It is, as Gadamer likes to say, "self-standing" and "conceptually inexhaustible" (GW8.1/PH96). More than this, however, the eminent text is one that seems to address us specifically in virtue of the way in which our own self-understanding becomes involved in our attempts to interpret it. So we cannot put it aside or forget it without a sense of self-alienation. It is a part of our remembrance. Cf. *Wahrheit und Methode* on the nature of the classical: "The classical . . . , as Hegel says, is 'that which is self-significant (selbst bedeutende) and hence also self-interpretive (selber Deutende).' But that ultimately means that the classical preserves itself precisely *because* it is significant in itself and interprets itself; i.e., it speaks in such a way that it is not a statement about what is past—documentary evidence that still needs to be interpreted—rather, it says something to the present as if it were said specifically to it. What we call 'classical' does not first require the overcoming of historical distance, for in its own constant mediation it overcomes this distance by itself" (WM273–74/TM289–90).

2. See "Zu Poetik und Hermeneutik" (GW8.58–69), part one of which is subtitled "Lyrik als Paradigma der Moderne." The lyric for Gadamer is the paradigm of the modern work of art precisely because it is "hermetic": its intelligibility is no longer self-evident but is constituted by the interlocution of sound and sense. See "Dichten und Deuten" (1961): "Compared with all other art forms, the poetic work of art possesses as language *[als sprachliches]* a characteristic indeterminacy *[eine spezifische, offene Unbestimmtheit]*. The unity of form that is so characteristic of the poetic work, as it is of every other kind, is sensuously present, and to that extent cannot be reduced to the mere intention of meaning" (GW8.21/RB70). See also "Vom Verstummen des Bildes" (1965): "If we consider the rich, colorful, and resplendent eloquence that speaks to us so clearly and fluently from the classical periods of painting represented in our museums, and compare

it with the creative art of our own time, we certainly have the impression of speechlessness" (GW8.315/RB83). And see "Die Aktualität des Schönen" (1977): "The poetry of our time has reached the limits of intelligible meaning and perhaps the greatest achievements of the greatest writers are themselves marked by a tragic speechlessness in the face of the unsayable" (GW8.100/RB9). The poetry of Paul Celan is for Gadamer the *locus classicus* of this problem of the speechlessness of modernity. The problem for Gadamer is how a work that is to all appearances "speechless" can continue to "address" us. See "Verstummen die Dichter?" (1970): "The question is not whether the poets are silent, but whether our ear is acute enough to hear" (GW9.363/EPH78).

3. *The Art of Poetry*, trans. Denise Folliot (New York: Vintage Books, 1961), pp. 170–71. Cf. Gadamer, "Philosophie und Literatur" (1981): "Paul Valéry splendidly portrays the difference between the poetic word and the everyday word by comparing them respectively to the old gold coin and today's paper bill. It was still taught in our schools that if you take a hammer and pound on a twenty dollar gold piece so that one can no longer see the minting and go to a jeweler, he will give you twenty dollars again. The coin is its own value—its value is not only printed on it. And this is the poem, namely, language which not only signifies something, but is itself that which it signifies. Today's paperbill is worth nothing; its only meaning is its appearance, allowing it to perform its commercial function" (GW8.248–49); "Philosophy and Literature," trans. Anthony J. Steinbock, *Man and World*, 18 (1985), 249–50. See also "Philosophie und Poesie" (1977) (GW8.233/RB132).

4. See "Grenzen der Sprache" (1985), GW8.350–61, esp. p. 360: "Da ist Poesie, das lyrische Gedicht, die grosse Instanz für die Erfahrung der Eigenheit und der Fremdheit der Sprache."

5. See my discussion of the formalist-structuralist tradition in *Modern Poetry and the Idea of Language: A Critical and Historical Study* (New Haven: Yale University Press, 1974), pp. 71–100.

6. See *The Philosophical Discourse of Modernity*, trans. Frederick Lawrence (Cambridge: MIT Press, 1990), esp. pp. 207–10.

7. See *Moral Consciousness and Communicative Action*, trans. Christian Lenhardt and Shierry Weber Nicholsen (Cambridge: MIT Press, 1990), pp. 17–20.

8. *Imaginations*, ed. Webster Schott (New York: New Directions, 1970), p. 145.

9. This is an insight pressed enthusiastically by Stanley Cavell, who draws some inspiration from Heidegger. See "The Uncanniness of the Ordinary," *In Quest of the Ordinary: Lines of Skepticism and Romanticism* (Chicago: Chicago University Press, 1988), pp. 153–78.

10. See "The Task of the Translator" (1923), *Illuminations*, trans. Harry Zohn (New York: Schocken Books, 1968), p. 80.

11. Williams's *Paterson* (1946–58), for example, is a poem made out of every sort of discourse imaginable, not all of it of Williams's own composition. Here is an excerpt from Book Five, Section II, which also contains a poem by Sappho and a letter from Ezra Pound. It consists of an interview that Williams gave, and Stephen Fredman tells me that the interviewer was Mike Wallace:

(Q. Mr. Williams, can you tell me, simply, what poetry is?
A. Well . . . I would say that poetry is language charged with emotion. It's works, rhythmically organized. . . . A poem is a complete little universe. It exists separately. Any poem that has worth expresses the whole life of the poet. It gives a view of what the poet is.
Q. All right, look at this part of a poem by E. E. Cummings, another great American poet:

> (im)c-a-t(mo)
> b,i;l:e
> FallleA
> ps!fl
> OattumblI
> sh?dr
> IftwhirlF
> (UL) (lY)
> &&&

Is this poetry?

A. I would reject it as a poem. It may be, to him, a poem. But I would reject it. I can't understand it. He's a serious man. So I struggle very hard with it—and I get no meaning at all.

Q. You get no meaning? But here's part of a poem you yourself have written: . . . "2 partridges/2 mallard ducks/ a Dungeness crab/24 hours out/of the Pacific/and 1 live-frozen/trout/from Denmark . . . " Now that sounds just like a fashionable grocery list.

A. It is a fashionable grocery list.

Q. Well—is it poetry?

A. We poets have to talk in a language which is not English. It is the American idiom. Rhythmically it's organized as a sample of the American idiom. It has as much originality as jazz. If you say "2 partridges, 2 mallard ducks, a Dungeness crab"—if you treat that rhythmically, ignoring the practical sense, it forms a jagged pattern. It is, to my mind, poetry.

Q. But if you don't "ignore the practical sense" . . . you agree that it is a fashionable grocery list.

A. Yes. Anything is good material for poetry. Anything. I've said it time and time again.

Q. Aren't we supposed to understand it?

A. There is a difference of poetry and the sense. Sometimes modern poets ignore sense completely. That's what makes some of the difficulty. . . . The audience is confused by the shape of the words.

Q. But shouldn't a word mean something when you see it?

A. In prose, an English word means what it says. In poetry, you're listening to two things . . . you're listening to the sense, the common sense of what it says. But it says more. That is the difficulty.

. . . .) (*Paterson* [New York: New Directions, 1963], pp. 261–62)

Notice again the link between poetry and listening. Poetry is not original creation but a listening to the language that we speak.

12. *The Age of Huts* (New York: Roof Books, 1986), p. 49. See Stephen Fredman, *Poet's Prose: The Crisis in American Verse*, 2nd edition (Cambridge: Cambridge University Press, 1990).

13. See "Disappearance of the Word, Appearance of the Word," *The New Sentence* (New York: ROOF Books, 1989), pp. 7–18.

14. *La part du feu* (Paris: Gallimard, 1949), pp. 316–17; *The Gaze of Orpheus*, trans. Lydia Davis (Barrytown: Station Hill Press, 1981), p. 46.

15. See Gadamer's discussion of the "speculative structure" of language in *Truth and Method* (WD441–46/TM465–70, esp. 445/70). Poetry is something like a shake-up of the use of language in which there is always a reversal of subjectivity that prevents us from going on as before.

16. Michael Davidson, "The Prose of Fact," *Hills*, 6–7 (Spring 1980), p. 166.

17. See William Paulson, *The Noise of Culture: Literary Texts in a World of Information* (Ithaca: Cornell University Press, 1988), esp. pp. 80–100. Fredric Jameson connects the "materialization" of the signifier in contemporary poetry and art with schizophrenia in order to make a point about Late Capitalism, in "Postmodernism and Consumer Society," *The Anti-Aesthetic: Essays on Postmodern Culture*, ed. Hal Foster (Port Townsend, Wa.: Bay Press, 1983), esp. pp. 120–22.

18. See "Das Wesen der Sprache," *Unterwegs zur Sprache* (Pfullingen: Günther Neske, 1959), p. 161; "The Nature of Language," trans. Peter D. Hertz (New York: Harper & Row, 1971), p. 59.

19. Maurice Blanchot observes, as part of his nearly lifelong argument with Emmanuel Levinas, that it is language that opens up the site of alterity. Language is the other of all others or the relation of foreignness as such (what Blanchot calls "the relation of the third kind"). Only in virtue of the radical exteriority opened up by the "experience of language" is such a thing as an ethical relation in Levinas's sense possible. See Blanchot, *L'entretien infini* (Paris: Gallimard, 1969), esp. p. 94; *The Infinite Conversation*, trans. Susan Hanson (Minneapolis: University of Minnesota Press, 1993), p. 66.

20. See Michel Foucault, *Les mots et les choses: une archéologie des sciences humaines* (Paris: Gallimard, 1966), pp. 307–13; *The Order of Things: An Archeology of the Human Sciences*, 1973), pp. 294–300.

21. Cf. "Philosophie und Poesie," where Gadamer takes up
the question, "Was ist Sprache in der Philosophie?" (GW8.237/
RB137). For Gadamer, *poésie pure* is a limit-concept. Its philosophical equivalent is Hegel's concept of the dialectic conceived
as speculation or the "mirror-play of the categories." "These
categories represent boundaries that bind and delimit in the
literal sense of the word *Horos* [the Greek word for boundary
and also for definition]. They are boundaries that are only defined reciprocally within the totality of the concept, and they
only represent the whole truth of the concept when they are all
taken together. Such speculative propositions mirror the *Aufhebung*
or sublation of their own immanent positing. They are like the
sayings of Heraclitus which express the One, the sole wisdom,
in a contradictory form *[Sie heissen spekulative Sätze, Spiegelsätze,
wie Heraklits Sprüche, die im Gegensatz das Eine, das Weise (en
ton sophon) sagen]*. They preserve the thought within themselves
by recovering it from all externalization in such a way that it is
reflected 'into itself.' The language of philosophy is a language
that sublates itself, saying nothing and turning towards the whole
at one and the same time" (GW8.238/RB138).

22. Here I've amended the English text, which misprints
"stronger" for "stranger."

23. See Herman Rapaport, *Heidegger and Derrida: Reflections on Time and Language* (Lincoln: University of Nebraska
Press, 1989), pp. 137–38.

24. This refusal belongs to the being or truth of the work
and to the being of beings as well. See Gadamer, "Die Wahrheit
des Kunstwerkes": "truth is not simply the mere presence of a
being, so that it stands, as it were, over against its correct representation. Such a concept of being unconcealed would presup-
pose the subjectivity of the Dasein that represents beings. But
beings are not correctly defined in their Being if they are defined
merely as objects of possible representation. Rather, it belongs
just as much to their Being that they withhold themselves. As
unconcealed, truth has in itself an inner tension and ambiguity.
Being contains something like a 'hostility to its own presence,'
as Heidegger says" (GW3.259–60/HW107).

25. In his discussion in *Truth and Method* of the speculative
character of poetic language. Gadamer quotes the passage from

Hölderlin that seems to have inspired Heidegger's characterization of *Dichtung*, and goes on to clarify the link between *Dichtung* and *Poesie*. Gadamer writes:

> Hölderlin has shown that finding the language of a poem involves totally dissolving all customary words and modes of expression. "In that the poet feels himself seized in his whole inner and outer life by the pure tone of his original sensation and he looks about him in his world, it is new and unknown to him, the sum of all his experiences, his knowledge, his intuitions and memories, art and nature, as it presents itself within and without him; everything is present to him as if for the first time, for this very reason ungrasped, undetermined, dissolved into sheer material and life. And it is supremely important that he does not at this moment accept anything as given, does not start from anything positive, that nature and art, as he has learned to know and see them, do not *speak* before a language is there for *him*." (WM445–46/TM470)

26. See Christopher Fynsk, "Poetic Relation: Celan's Bremen Address," *The Poetry of Paul Celan*, ed. Haskell M. Block (New York: Peter Lang, 1991), pp. 22–29, esp. p. 25. An expanded version of this essay, now including an interesting commentary on "Der Meridian," appears in *Word Traces: Readings of Paul Celan*, ed. Aris Fioretos (Baltimore: Johns Hopkins University Press, 1994), pp. 159–84.

27. A "language of *Erfahrung*"? Heidegger speaks of undergoing an "experience with language [mit der Sprache eine Erfahrung zu machen]," where "undergoing an experience with something—be it a thing, a person, or a god—means that this something befalls us, strikes us, comes over us, overwhelms and transforms us" (US159/OWL57). We may imagine Celan reversing this event, that is, language for Celan is something that can undergo an experience with history and be overwhelmed and transformed just in the sense that it can never go back to the way it was; it is always marked by the events it lives through. Celan helps to show the marks, and perhaps that is what poets are for in a destitute time.

28. Quoted by Israel Chalfen, *Paul Celan: A Biography of his Youth*, trans. Maximilian Bleyleben (New York: Persea Books, 1991), p. 4.

29. Gilles Deleuze and Félix Guattari, *Kafka: Toward a Minor Literature*, trans. Dana Polan (Minneapolis: University of Minnesota Press, 1986), p. 26.

30. It needs to be emphasized that for poets like Celan the corporeality of language—the idea that poetry is the flesh and breath of language—is not a metaphor. The American poet Charles Bernstein puts it plainly in his *ars poetica*, "Artifice of Absorption" (1985–87):

> The *intersection*
> of absorption and impermeability is precisely
> *flesh*,
> as Merleau-Ponty uses this term
> to designate the intersection of the visible
> & the invisible. This
> is the philosophical interior
> of my inquiry—that absorption and impermeability
> are the warp & woof of poetic composition—
> an intertwining or chiasm whose locus
> is the flesh of the word. Yet writing re-
> verses the dynamic Merleau-Ponty out-
> lines for the visible & the invisible:
> for it is the invisible of writing
> that is imagined to be absorbed
> while the visible of writing usually goes unheard
> or is silenced. The visibility of words
> as a precondition of reading
> necessitates that words obtrude impermeably into
> the world—this
> impermeability makes a reader's absorption
> in words possible. The *thickness*
> of words ensures that whatever
> of their physicality is erased, or engulfed, in
> the process of semantic projection,
> a residue
> tenaciously in-

heres that will not be sublimated
away. Writing is not a thin film
of expendable substitutions that, when reading, falls
away
like scales
to reveal a meaning. The tenacity of
writing's thickness, like the body's
flesh, is ineradicable, yet mortal. It is
the intrusion
of words into the visible
that marks
writing's own absorption in the world.
To literally put words into Merleau-Ponty's mouth:
The thickness of writing between
the reader & the poem is constitutive for the poem
of its visibility & for the reader
of the outer limit of his or her absorption
in the poem; it is not an obstacle
between them, it is their means
of communication. The thickness of writing,
far from rivaling that of the world,
is on the contrary the sole
means it has to go to the heart of things
by making itself part
of the material world, absorbed
by it.

Notice what Bernstein is saying: it is the thickness of poetry, the impermeability of its flesh, that makes possible the dialogue between poem and readers. *A Poetics* (Cambridge: Harvard University Press, 1992), pp. 86–87.

31. See Maurice Blanchot, *L'entretien infini*, pp. 613–19. esp. p. 614, where writing is understood as an event of *désoeuvrement*:

Unworking *[désoeuvrement]* is at work, but does not produce the work. Thus when we analyze and comment on the work, we have a tendency either to determine this movement of unworking as the originality of a new order, one harmony breaking with another, or to grasp it as an autonomous principle of the work's engendering, its unity at work, whereas worklessness [*désoeuvrement*] is always outside the work: that which has not let itself be put to work, the always un-unified irregularity (the non-structure) that makes it so that the work relates to something other than itself, not because it says or enunciates (recites, reproduces) this other thing—the "real"—but because it only says itself in saying this *other* thing, saying it through this distance and difference, this play between words and things that is also between things and things and between one language and another (*The Infinite Conversation*, p. 418).

32. Celan makes the following comment:

Please note, ladies and gentlemen: "One would like to be a Medusa's head" to . . . seize the natural as the natural by means of art!

One would like to, by the way, not: *I* would [Man *möchte heisst es hier freilich, nicht:* ich *möchte]*" (GW3.192/CP42).

As if the "I" could not be used by an artist, which is an old story, but not Celan's. For Celan the "I" cannot be used hypothetically or interchangeably; it is not a universal. It is untranslatable. So he makes a point of distinguishing Lenz, the hero of Büchner's *Lenz* (a fragment), and the historical Lenz, "the Lenz who on the 20th of January was walking through the mountains," he—not the artist thinking about art—he as an 'I'" (GW3.194/CP46). See Jacques Derrida, *Schibboleth* (Paris: Galilée, 1986), esp. pp. 18–28.

33. Gerhard Buhr, *Celans Poetik* (Göttingen: Vandenhoeck & Ruprecht, 1976), pp. 64–77; Holger Pausch, *Paul Celan* (Berlin: Otto Bess, 1981), pp. 49–51; David Brierly, *"Der Meridian": Ein Versuch zur Poetik und Dichtung Paul Celans* (Frankfurt: Peter Lang, 1984), pp. 156–83.

34. Levinas, *Autrement qu'être ou au-dela de l'essence* (The Hague: Martinus Nijhoff, 1974), p. 276; *Otherwise than Being,*

trans. Alphonso Lingis (The Hague: Martinus Nijhoff, 1978), p. 178.

35. See Krzysztof Ziarek, *Inflected Language: Toward a Hermeneutics of Nearness: Heidegger, Levinas, Stevens, Celan* (Albany: SUNY Press, 1994), p. 183, on Levinas's appropriation of Celan's metaphorics of the breath in *Otherwise than Being*.

36. See Olson, "Projective Verse," *Selected Writings*, ed. Robert Creeley (New York: New Directions, 1966), esp. pp. 16–22.

37. Derrida tries to clarify this by saying that the poem is of the same ontology as the date or the *shibboleth*; it is absolutely singular and at the same time never itself. So, as Derrida says: "The date is mad." See *Schibboleth pour Paul Celan*, p. 68.

38. See Heidegger, *Gelassenheit* (Pfullingen: Günther Neske, 1959), p. 24.

39. *Gelassenheit* is perhaps as much a political as an ethical concept because the condition of openness that it entails is an acceptance or acknowledgment of the other's freedom (the freedom of things and of beings). This freedom is ontological rather than subjective; that is, it is not the freedom of another subject, freedom as mastery or harmony, but just the anarchic condition of openness in which the singularity or non-identity of things can take place or, as one should say, can go on. Jean-Luc Nancy calls it "the free dissemination of existence"; it is "the an-archy . . . of a singular and thus in essence plural arising whose being *as being* is neither ground, nor element, nor reason, but truth, which would amount to saying, under the circumstances, freedom." See *L'expérience de la liberté* (Paris: Galilée, 1988), p. 16–17; *The Experience of Freedom*, trans. Bridget McDonald (Stanford: Stanford University Press, 1993), p. 13. Freedom in this sense is not a property or power; it is the separation of existence from essence, identity, or ground. Nor is this separation anything negative. Nancy thinks of it in terms of a "generosity" or "prodigality" of being in which the singular is allowed to exist independently of any justification, without ground or "without why." Freedom is just this groundlessness. Nancy associates it with the *il y a* understood in Heidegger's sense of the free gift rather than in Levinas's sense of the horror of being (ExL77/EF55). Nancy's metaphor for freedom is that of "a prodigality of *bursts [d'éclats]*"; "freedom is essentially *bursting*" (ExL80/

EF57). "It is a bursting or singularity of existence, which means existence deprived of essence and delivered to this inessentiality, to its own surprise as well as to its own decision, to its own indecision as well as to its own generosity" (ExL81/EF57). As if there were an internal link between freedom and the excessive.

Freedom is not subjective, but it is accessible to subjectivity in some familiar and even comic or utopian ways. In a splendid paragraph Nancy writes:

> "Freedom" cannot avoid combining, in a unity that has only its own generosity as an index, the values of impulse, chance, luck, the unforeseen, the decided, the game, the discovery, conclusion, dazzlement, the syncope, courage, reflection, rupture, terror, suture, abandonment, hope, caprice, rigor, the arbitrary. Also: laughter, tears, scream, word, rapture, chill, shock, energy, sweetness. . . . Freedom is also wild freedom, the freedom of indifference, the freedom of choice, availability, the free game, freedom of comportment, of air, of love, of a free time where time begins again. (ExL79–80/EF56)

But prior to these freedoms there is the ontological condition of freedom that calls for thinking—thinking as responsibility rather than ratiocination. "Freedom," Nancy says, "is the leap into existence, in which existence is discovered as such, and this discovery is thinking"—thinking *as experience:* "a thought other than understanding, reason, knowledge, contemplation, philosophy, other finally than thought itself. The *other* thought of all thought—which is not the Other of thought, nor the thought of the Other, but that by which thought thinks—is the burst of freedom" (ExL82–83/EF58–59).

Freedom is a limit-concept. So the fact that we lack a theory or vocabulary for this event in which the singular occurs is not a deficiency but part of the decorum of freedom itself. The task of thinking is not conceptualization but responsiveness, openness, and acknowledgment—"the recognition of the freedom of being in its singularity" (ExL17/EF13). In a comparable way the reserve or fragmentariness of Celan's discourse in "Der Meridian" is not a deficiency. Like Blanchot, Celan tries to articulate a poetics of non-identity, of singularity and irreducibility, that remains on the hither side of theory or the clarification of concepts. Poetry is freedom: without why, without ground, unnameable—perhaps this is already saying too much (GW3.177/ CP25).

40. See Thomas Sparr, "Celans Poetik des Raums," *Celans Poetik des hermetischen Gedichts* (Heidelberg: Carl Winter, 1989), pp. 137–53, on Celan's poetics of *Ortlosigkeit* (p. 149).

41. See *Mons propres* (Paris: Fata Morgana, 1976), pp. 49–56. See Véronique Fóti's Levinasian readings of Celan, who is again enlisted in a campaign against Heidegger, *Heidegger and the Poets: Poiesis, Sophia, Techne* (Atlantic Highlands, N. J.: Humanities Press, 1992), pp. 99–114 and esp. 114–24. Cf. the "post-ethical" allegory of Celan's "Todesfuge" by John D. Caputo, with commentary, in *Against Ethics: Contributions to a Poetics of Obligation with Constant Reference to Deconstruction* (Bloomington: Indiana University Press, 1993), pp. 176–86. For a very different approach to Celan in the context of Levinas and Heidegger, see Krzysztof Ziarek, *Inflected Language*, esp. pp. 133–60.

42. See *La poésie comme expérience* (Paris: Christian Bourgois, 1986), pp. 97–98.

43. *L'Entretien infini*, p. 76; *The Infinite Conversation*, p. 53. See also pp. 98–105/71–74. For Blanchot, beyond the relation of meaning and beyond the ethical relation there is also, in writing, "a relation of the third kind" that is opened up by the experience of language. This relation is, one might say, not ethical but topological: a relation that can only be clarified in terms of an open and indeterminate space. Celan seems closer to Blanchot than to Levinas in this respect.

44. *La poésie comme expérience*, pp. 94–96. In "Der Meridian" Celan writes:

This "still-here" of the poem can only be found in the work of poets who do not forget that they speak from an angle of reflection which is their own existence, their own physicality *[dass er unter dem Neigungswinkel seines Daseins, dem Neigungswinkel seiner Kreatürlichkeit spricht]*.

This shows the poem yet more clearly as one person's language becomes shape and, essentially, a presence in the present [*Dann wäre das Gedicht— deutlicher noch als bisher—gestaltgewordene Sprache eines Einzelnen,—und seinem innersten Wesen nach Gegenwart und Präsenz.* (GW3.197–98/CP49)

Lacoue-Labarthe, like Levinas, effaces the creatureliness incorporated by the language of the poem.

45. *Mandelstam: Critical Prose and Letters*, trans. Jay Gary Harris and Constance Link, ed. Jane Gary Harris (Ann Arbor: Ardis, 1979), p. 73. There are good discussions of this matter by Martine Broda in *Dans la main de personne*, pp. 61–94.

46. See the chapter on "The Tragedy of Hermeneutical Experience," in Gerald L. Bruns, *Hermeneutics Ancient and Modern* (New Haven: Yale University Press, 1992), pp. 179–94.

47. In "Phänomenologischer und semantischer Zugang zu Celan," a paper presented to the Heidelburg Celan Colloquium in 1991, Gadamer says that he does not approach Celan as a specialist. He remains, he says, "the outsider, aspiring merely to reconstruct again and again the texts of poems which move and speak to me. This is not the task of scholarly analysis, but remains the ultimate point of any scholarly concern with art" (GW9.461). There is no doubt that philological and historical descriptions of the text are foundational for rigorous scholarship. But they cannot replace the hermeneutical experience in which the text addresses me across the distance that separates me from it. This distance is not one that can be filled in by information; it is the difference from myself that only the voice of another can place before me.

48. Derrida, *Schibboleth*, pp. 60–61; "A Shibboleth for Paul Celan," trans. Joshua Wilner, *Word Traces: Readings of Paul Celan* (Baltimore: Johns Hopkins University Press, 1994), pp. 35–36.

49. Gadamer adds, with respect to the way narratives remain in excess of their telling and retelling: "To leave an enormous amount open seems to me the essence of a fruitful fable and myth. Thanks precisely to its open indeterminacy, myth is able to produce constant new invention from within itself, with the thematic horizon continuously shifting in different directions.

Derrida on Celan
word Traces

(We need only think of the many attempts to treat the Faust theme, from Marlowe to Paul Valéry)" (WM471/TM498–99).

50. *The Journal of Philosophy*, 61, no. 19 (October 1964), 581.

51. See John Felstiner, " 'Clawed into Each Other': Jewish vs. Christian Memory in Paul Celan's 'Tenebrae,' " *TriQuarterly* 87 (Spring/Summer 1993), 193–203.

52. *Totalité et infini: Essai sur l'extériorité* (The Hague: Martinus Nijhoff, 1961; rpt. Paris: Kluwer Academic, 1971), p. 69; *Totality and Infinity: An Essay on Exteriority*, trans. Alphonso Lingis (The Hague: Martinus Nijhoff, 1969), p. 72.

53. "The Book of Destruction," in *Probing the Limits of Representation: Nazism and the "Final Solution,"* ed. Saul Friedlander (Cambridge, Mass.: Harvard University Press, 1992), p. 326.

Abbreviations

Paul Celan

CP   *Collected Prose.* Trans. Rosemarie Waldrop. New York: The Sheep Meadow Press, 1986.

GW   *Gesammelte Werke.* 5 vols. Ed. Beda Allemann and Stefan Reichert. Frankfurt: Suhrkamp, 1983.

PPC   *Poems of Paul Celan.* Trans. Michael Hamburger. New York: Persea Books, 1988.

Hans-Georg Gadamer

DD   *Dialogue and Deconstruction: The Gadamer-Derrida Encounter.* Ed. Diane Michelfelder and Richard Palmer. Albany: SUNY Press, 1989.

EPH   *On Education, Poetry, and History: Applied Hermeneutics.* Trans. Lawrence Schmidt and Monica Reuss. Albany: SUNY Press, 1992.

GW   *Gesammelte Werke.* 10 vols. Tübingen: J. C. B. Mohr (Paul Siebeck), 1986.

HW   *Heidegger's Ways.* Trans. John W. Stanley. Albany: SUNY Press, 1994.

PA   *Philosophical Apprenticeships.* Trans. Robert R. Sullivan. Cambridge: MIT Press, 1985.

PH   *Philosophical Hermeneutics.* Trans. David Linge. Berkeley: University of California Press, 1976.

RB   *The Relevance of the Beautiful and Other Essays.* Trans. Nicholas Walker. Cambridge: Cambridge University Press, 1986.

TM   *Truth and Method.* 2nd rev. ed. Trans. Joel Weinsheimer and Donald G. Marshall. New York: Crossroad, 1989.

WM   *Wahrheit und Methode: Grundzüge einer philosophischen Hermeneutik.* 4th ed. Tübingen: J. C. B. Mohr (Paul Siebeck), 1975.

Martin Heidegger

GA   *Gesamtausgabe.* Frankfurt: Vittorio Klostermann, 1977.

OWL *On the Way to Language.* Trans. Peter Hertz. New York: Harper and Row, 1971.

PLT *Poetry, Language, Thought.* Trans. Albert Hofstadter. New York: Harper and Row, 1971.

US   *Unterwegs zur Sprache.* Pfullingen: Günther Neske, 1959.

Editors' Preface

This book gathers all the major work by Hans-Georg Gadamer on Paul Celan. Gadamer published the book *Wer bin Ich und wer bist Du?* in 1973, and Suhrkamp republished that book, along with a new preface and appendix, in 1986. The translation is based mainly on the 1986 Suhrkamp text and the version that appears in Gadamer's *Gesammelte Werke*, because that later version includes some notes added by Gadamer.

The two essays that come after *Who am I and Who are You?* in this book follow up on the book-length commentary on Celan's poetry that Gadamer published in 1973. "Meaning and Concealment of Meaning in Paul Celan" was first published in 1975, and later collected into a book of essays that appeared in 1977. The last essay in this book, "A Phenomenological and Semantic Approach to Celan?," first came out in a collection of essays on Celan published in 1991, and has since been collected in Volume nine of Gadamer's *Gesammelte Werke*, along with the other two works that have been translated in this book.

Maintaining a chronological presentation of the book on Celan and the two essays seems important, since Gadamer views his attempts at understanding Celan's poetry as a cumulative effort, in which, among other things, he responds to and learns from other scholars who have attended to Celan's writings.

In translating the present volume, we have had the privilege of bearing witness to an extraordinary conversation between two supreme poetic and philosophical minds, a privilege equalled only by the challenge of attempting to listen in unobtrusively. Alas, despite our best efforts, we have not always been equal to the challenge.

Gadamer's intensely personal reflections on Celan, gleaned, as Gadamer tells us, while "listening earnestly in the damp wind," are an example of hermeneutic practice and as such, they are deeply intertwined with the poetry of this poet. This means that Gadamer's language is constantly shaped by his encounter with the poetry, and we have sought as much as possible to be true to the dialogic nature of the book.

Sometimes we were able to succeed in rendering the semantic resonances between the poetry and Gadamer's reading by choosing certain words and expressions—for example, "bearing witness," or "journeying"—even when English synonyms might have been more appropriate. Wherever necessary, we have noted such word-play for the reader in a bracket or footnote, although we have also tried to use these devices as sparingly as possible to avoid weighing the narrative down with "scholarly apparatus." In some cases, we made an effort to mirror the complexity of Gadamer's language even when doing so required stretching the boundaries of English grammar. While we hope the book reads with the natural flow of English, the reader will notice that certain constructions and syntactic configurations may require "reading again and again"—in which case, we trust we have asked no more than the poet himself.

The last sentence of the book is particularly revealing in this regard: " 'You' are what it testifies to ("Your" witness)—the intimate, unknown You which, for the I that here is the I of the poet as well as the reader, is its You, 'wholly, wholly real.' " What sounds grammatically awkward in English is no less so in the German. But Gadamer's formulation is deliberate, for the pronouns which follow the dash are set down in a chiasmic structure that reflects the movement of the entire book: the I and You of the poem break down the rigid barrier between poet and reader, allowing the poems to speak to all who read them, and allowing all who read them to speak them. Gadamer's reading turns on a movement which cannot be fixed in rigid determinations of who I and You are, a movement which follows the very evolution of I and You in poetic, social, historical, and spiritual terms. To smooth out the English syntax in this case thus seemed to have too high a price.

In a few instances, our ability to listen in could thus not but be obtrusive. No degree of syntactic straining can allow English, for example, to duplicate Gadamer's ability to alternate the use of upper- and lowercase with respect to the first person pronoun. Moreover, to bracket all such instances simply seemed too cumbersome. Here as elsewhere, we hope that the meaning of the larger context of the sentence and passage will provide the reader with enough support. Nevertheless, some of the semantic undercurrents had to be lost. For example, Gadamer's use of the word *treiben* throughout the book brings together many of Celan's important image spheres: the "production" of new shoots, the "driving" of undreamed dreams, the "propelling" of haphazard talk. Here, too, there was simply no way to listen in without preventing English from insisting on its own stylistic and semantic demands.

In this regard, it should be noted that we also have not refrained from abiding by American academic convention in using gender neutral formulations whenever possible, and especially when Gadamer is referring to the "reader," since such inclusiveness seems true to hermeneutic principle.

Hermeneutics tells us that a singular experience is also an instance of the general. Thus we can expect that while Gadamer's language is shaped by the encounter with Celan, it nevertheless invokes a number of general terms which will be recognizable by those acquainted with the philosophical tradition to which Gadamer belongs, as well as Gadamer's own hermeneutic theory. In translating words such as *Vorstellung, Anschauung, Begriff, Unbestimmtheit, Verstand,* and *Wirkungsgeschichtlich* we have therefore sought to abide by the conventions of philosophical and Gadamerian translation. We thus wish to acknowledge our debt to Robert Wallace, Don Marshall, Joel Weinsheimer, P. Christopher Smith, Monica Reuss, Dieter Misgeld, and Gerald Bruns, all of whom, among others, have done extraordinary work in introducing Gadamer to English readers. We have also included the German words in brackets, as well as a few explicatory notes, at points where we thought clarification or additional reference might be appreciated.

One set of terms is particularly important, however: those which Gadamer uses to describe the activity of reading poetry. Here, the reader may find it helpful to know some of our choices in advance: *Fügung* = "assemblage"; *Gefüge* = "framework"; *Gestalt* = "form"; *Gebilde* = "configuration"; *Rede* = "speech"; *Sinn* =

"meaning." By maintaining consistency in these choices, we have presumed a certain degree of precision in Gadamer's usage, which we will hope will become evident.

The word *vollziehen* presented a number of problems. Together with its related attributive and substantive forms *vollziehbar* and *Vollzug*, it is used by Gadamer to refer to understanding or following the meaning of poetic language. The German term carries associations with legal language—the "carrying out" of a sentence or a duty—as well as a literal sense of "pulling together." Thus it illuminates the sense in which interpretation involves a recognition of the "authority" of the text, and yet also involves active engagement on the part of the reader. We chose to render this set of terms with "complete" and its related forms "completion" and "completable." Other more precise alternatives such as "fulfillment," "execution," or "accomplishment" inevitably brought their own collection of distracting associations when used in their various forms. In order to preserve the consistency of Gadamer's usage, we thus settled on a word with a certain degree of syntactic and semantic neutrality.

As is well known, Celan's poetry itself presents the translator with enormous difficulties. Its syntactical boldness, its "assemblages" of words and meanings, its use of specific technical language, and its exquisite precision all make extraordinary demands on readers and translators. We were, however, fortunate to be able to consult the work of many before us, including Michael Hamburger, Joachim Neugroschel, Luitgard N. Wundheifer, Walter Billeter, and Pierre Joris. Their efforts helped make a path frought with risk a little easier to traverse.

Yet the problem is exacerbated in a book of this nature because Gadamer's readings often depend on structural and semantic features of the poems which simply can't be rendered in English. In the poem "Die Zahlen," for example, Gadamer emphasizes the concluding word *Besingt*, and for good reason, since the semantic, metrical, and structural weight that come together in it is a measure of the poem's precision, which the English reader cannot see. While we have sought to preserve at least the metrical weight of the line, Gadamer's reading may prove difficult to follow. In what he calls the "proem" to this cycle of poems, to cite another example, Gadamer considers the possibility of reading the first syllable of *Maulbeerbaum* as a reference to poetic pretensiousness, drawing on the literal meaning of the German word *Maul* ("mouth") and the term for "loud-mouth" *(Maulheld)*. So much conceivably depends on a morpheme nowhere to be found in the English "mulberry." In cases like this, the reader might wish to consult the German text which we have provided with the English translation.

Gadamer's reading also brings out the cyclical dimension of "Breath-crystal." Certain image spheres are invoked by Celan in this cycle again and again: the journey, the snow, the water, the land, and so on. Needless to say, we have tried to translate the poems in such a way as to convey their unity as a sequence, and yet this too proved impossible. For example, the word *geätzt* in the second poem, "Von Ungeträumtem," is related to *weggebeizt* in the last poem of the sequence in that both are technical terms in the field of graphics. The English "corroded" with which the first of this pair is translated does not adequately convey that relation, though it does pick up the chemical association with acids which Gadamer emphasizes. Another word, *Strahl*, appears in two poems, but is translated with different words: "stream" and "ray." As much as we would have liked to preserve consistency here, neither English equivalent could carry the full resonance of the German *Strahl*, and Gadamer's discussion would have sounded quite odd if we had forced the consistency. Thus the reader should know that in cases like these, our translation was guided by the principle of making sure that Gadamer's reading could be followed. And yet it would violate the spirit of Gadamer's endeavor for the reader not to refer to the original text whenever possible in putting Gadamer's reading "to the test."

Finally, we would like to make special mention of the generous assistance we received from Lawrence Schmidt, Dieter Misgeld, and especially Dennis J. Schmidt. Their thoughtful and expert advice contributed immeasurably to the improvement of our manuscript, and provided "irrefutable witness" to the seriousness and sincerity of the community of scholars interested in Gadamer's work. The Alexander von Humboldt-Stiftung provided Richard Heinemann with support during a significant portion of this project, as did the Laurentian University Research Fund for

Bruce Krajewski. We would also like to express our deepest gratitude to Hans-Georg Gadamer himself, who welcomed our project with warmth and enthusiasm.

Who Am I
and
Who Are You?

Foreword

Paul Celan's poems reach us, and yet we miss them. He himself understood his work as a "message in a bottle," and when over and over again somebody, first one, then another, finds and accepts this message, convinced that he or she is receiving some communication—what sort of a communication is it? What does it say? The present book does not claim to have achieved conclusive results through scholarly investigation, rather it attempts to put into words the experience of a reader whom such a message has reached. These are attempts at deciphering, as with written signs that have become almost illegible. No one doubts that something was there. One must ponder, guess, restore—until finally one will have deciphered, will read and hear—perhaps even correctly. Without such careful deciphering no one can believe that he or she is capable of saying or knowing anything about the message of these verses, let alone the language in which they are written. In bearing witness here to an extended acquaintanceship, this reader believes he has found "sense" in these dark characters—not always an unambiguous sense, not always a "complete" sense. In many cases, he has deciphered merely a few passages and offered some vague conjectures about how to mend the gaps of his understanding (not of the text). I am not speaking with—nor writing for—anyone who thinks he or she has already understood Celan's poems. That person does not know what understanding means in this case. On the other hand, it is a legitimate experience if another reader should find that he or she has "always already" understood these poems just as the author suggests. Whether that person is correct in believing this, or whether that person

simply hasn't noticed that the matter became clear while reading
my essay, either way something is gained. If the reader believes
that he or she has understood these poems differently and better,
still more is gained. At that point such a reply will move us all
along—closer to the poetic work.

It must be added that these interpretations were written
years ago for Paul Celan and delivered on various occasions, for
instance, at the Goethe House in New York in 1969. Now they
must stand alone and remain without answer. Yet since then,
many discussions with others, most recently at the Celan
Colloquium of the Goethe Institute in Paris in September 1972,
have contributed especially to clarifying the methodological aspect of understanding this poetry. This will be taken up in the
Epilogue.

Foreword to the
Revised Edition

I t is now over a decade since my little commentary to "Breath-crystal" appeared. I have not dared to check over all of my original essay—indeed, if I could draw on the same sharpness and vigor, a new book would result. I have limited myself to correcting mistakes and applying information I have become aware of since then. In particular, I have attempted here, in a second Epilogue, to consider the insights I have gleaned from critical observations. I have also looked through the variations to the sequence "Breath-crystal," with which I have since become familiar, and discussed the interesting aspects of these in the Epilogue. The new edition thus follows the old one almost word for word. Only with respect to the poem on page 115 have I written a complete revision, since here the acquisition of new information has enabled me to present better insights.

Who Am I and
Who Are You?

In the pure hand of the poet
water will cluster
                    —Goethe

I n his later volumes of poetry, Paul Celan increasingly moved
toward the breathless stillness of muted silence in words
which have become cryptic. In what follows, I will examine
a sequence of poems from the book *Breath-turn*, which was first
published in 1965 in a bibliophile's edition under the title "Breath-
crystal." Each of the poems has its place in a sequence, and read
within this context, each poem achieves a certain measure of
precision—but the entire sequence of these poems is hermetically encoded. What are they about? Who is speaking?

Even so, every poem in this sequence is a configuration of
unambiguous precision; and while they are not transparent, nor
articulated with direct clarity, neither are they veiled, or capable
of being interpreted arbitrarily. This is the experience of reading
which awaits the patient reader. The reader who is interested in
understanding and decoding hermetic lyrics must clearly not be
hurried. Such a reader need not be scholarly, or especially learned.
He or she must simply try to keep listening.

The special instructions which a poet can give about his
encoded creations is always rather precarious (of Celan it is said

that when the desire for such instructions was occasionally directed to him, he tried to satisfy it in a friendly manner). But is it necessary to have knowledge of what the poet himself thought about a poem? All that matters is what the poem actually says, not what its author intended and perhaps did not know how to say. Of course a hint from the author regarding the raw material of his subject 'matter' can be useful even for a perfectly self-contained poem, and can guard against misunderstanding. But such hints remain a dangerous crutch. When a poet shares his private and occasional motives, he basically displaces what has been balanced out as a poetic configuration toward the side of the private and contingent—which, in any case, is not even there. Of course the task of interpreting hermetically encoded poems can often be quite perplexing. But should one go astray, after repeated lingering with a poem one always becomes aware of one's mistake, and even if one's understanding remains uncertain or approximate, it is the poem which speaks, and not an individual in the privacy of his experiences or sensations. A poem that withholds itself and does not permit further clarity always seems more meaningful to me than whatever clarity one might obtain from the poet's simple assurances about his intentions.

Thus while it is uncertain in these poems who I and You are, one should not ask the poet. Is it love poetry? Is it religious poetry? Is it a dialogue of the soul with itself? The poet doesn't know. One is better off finding enlightenment through the methods of comparative literary study, and especially through considering related poetic forms. Yet such enlightenment can be found only under certain conditions: only when the formal pattern used is appropriate, and when what is compared is genuinely comparable. In order to be sure, one needs more than a command over the methods of literary study. Only the given configuration in the polyvalence of its structure can decide which of the possibilities of subsumption available for comparison is suitable, and whether it possesses even limited explicatory power. With respect to Celan's poems, and the question posed here about who I and You are, I generally do not expect much help from a theoretical framework. All understanding presupposes an answer to this question, or better, a preliminary insight superior to the formulation of the question.

Readers of lyric poetry always already understand in a certain sense who I is. Not just in the trivial sense of knowing that it is always the poet who speaks, rather than a speaking person introduced by him. Beyond that, readers also know what the poet-I actually is. For the I pronounced in a lyric poem cannot be conclusively limited to the I of the poet, which would be different from that of the I-pronouncing reader. Even when the poet is "cradled in his characters," expressly separating himself from the "instantly mocking" crowd, it is as if he no longer means himself, but rather also includes the reader in his I-character, separating him or her from the crowd in the same way he knows himself to be. This is especially true with Celan, where "I," "you," and "we" are pronounced in an utterly direct, shadowy-uncertain and constantly changing way. This I is not only the poet, but even more so "that individual" *[jener Einzelne]*, as Kierkegaard named the one who is each of us.

Does this idea also contain an answer to the question of who You is here, who, like the speaking "I," is addressed directly and uncertainly in almost all the poems of this cycle? The You is the addressee as such. That is the general semantic function, and one must then ask how the movement of meaning in poetic speech fulfills this function. Is it meaningful to ask who this You is? As in the sense of: is it someone close to me? My neighbor? Or perhaps God, the closest and most distant of all? This cannot be determined. Who the You is cannot be determined because it hasn't been determined. The address has an aim, but it has no object—other than perhaps whoever faces up to the address by answering. Even the Christian love commandment does not determine the extent to which one's neighbor is God, or God one's neighbor. The You is only so much and so little I as the I I is.

This does not mean that in this sequence of poems which here pronounces I and You, the difference between the I that speaks and the You that is addressed is blurred; nor that as the cycle progresses, the I does not obtain a degree of precision. Thus we will hear, for example, of forty life-trees, an allusion to how old the I is. But even then it is crucial that the reader-I be willing to take the position of the poet-I and be equally implicated, and that in this way the You acquires precision. In the entire sequence the only exception appears to be the four verses set in parentheses by the poet, which stand out because of their almost epic diction. In contrast to all the others, their inability to be easily generalized is precisely what makes them seem almost incidental. Thus everything remains open for us now to make a trial approach to the poems of this Celan sequence. We do not know at the outset, on the basis of any distanced overview or preview, what I or You means here, or whether I is the I of the poet referring to himself, or the I that is each of us. That is what we must learn.

CONSOLED YOU may
welcome me with snow:
whenever I strode through the summer
shoulder to shoulder with the mulberry tree,
its youngest leaf
screamed.

DU DARFST mich getrost
mit Schnee bewirten:
sooft ich Schulter an Schulter
mit dem Maulbeerbaum schritt durch den Sommer,
schrie sein jüngstes
Blatt.

This is like a proem to the entire sequence. It is a difficult text which begins with strange directness. The poem is controlled by a sharp contrast. Snow makes everything the same, freezes and stills. Yet here it is not only accepted, but welcomed. This is because the summer, which remains behind the speaker, was apparently impossible to endure in the profusion of its germinating, budding, and blooming. Clearly, no actual summer lies behind the speaker, just as the You addressed in the poem does not mean winter or make an offer of real snow. Apparently it was a time of abundance, in contrast to which the sterile deprivation of the winter works like an act of charity. The speaker strode through the summer shoulder to shoulder with the tirelessly germinating mulberry tree. The mulberry tree here is undoubtedly the emblem of germinating energy, and the constantly lush production of new growth is a symbol of an insatiable thirst for life. Unlike other shrubbery, the mulberry tree produces fresh leaves not only in the spring, but throughout the entire summer. I don't think it's correct to recall the old metaphorical tradition of baroque poetry. Admittedly, Paul Celan was a *poeta doctus*, but more importantly, he had an extraordinary knowledge of nature. Heidegger told me that up in the Black Forest, Celan knew more about the plants and animals than he did.

Already here, in one's first approach to the poem, one must understand as concretely as possible. This means correctly accounting for the poet's awareness of language, since he not only uses words in their clear reference to objects, but also constantly plays with the meanings and associations that sound in them. One can thus ask whether the poet here is playing with the syllable "mouth" *[Maul,* from *Maulbeerbaum]* by referring to the loudmouth *[Maulheld des Wortes],* whose shouting he can no longer bear. Even so, our primary consideration remains precise coherence and must be met first. The plant name "mulberry tree" is quite common, and if one follows the poetic context in which the name occurs, it is clear that the poem refers neither to the mulberry nor to the mouth, but to the new verdure which sprouts tirelessly on the mulberry tree throughout the entire summer. Any further transposition must derive its direction of meaning from this fact. And we will see that this further transposition of what is said points ultimately to the sphere of silence, or the most austere speech. But evidently here the parallel with the mulberry tree points not to the mulberries, but to the sprouting lushness of the foliage. The double meaning of "mouth" is thus not supported by the context, but it is the scream of the leaf which grounds the movement of meaning. This is sharply accentuated in the text in the last word of the poem. It is thus the leaf and not the berry which conveys the transposition into what is actually said. In one level of the overtones one might then be led back from the scream to link the syllable "mouth" with speech. After all, there is indeed the loudmouth. And in this context, that might suggest all vain and empty speaking and writing of poetry. But that doesn't change the fact that the word "mouth" does not occur as an independent semantic unit [Sinneinheit] but rather merely as the initial signification of mulberry tree. The berry of *mouth [Beere des Maules]*, rather than the mouth's flower [Blume des Mundes] does not appear to me to be the right path for undertaking the transition from the first level of saying to the transpositional movement of expression [die Transpositions-bewegung des Besagens] which such a multifaceted poem actuates.*

There is thus all the more reason to ask what the poem "expresses," that is, toward what completion of meaning the text aims. Let us consider a few details: "shoulder to shoulder." To stride shoulder to shoulder with the mulberry tree apparently means not lagging behind, putting no stop to growth—which in this case would mean restful contemplation.** Moreover, one must observe that it says "whenever" [so oft]. This emphasis on a repeated path suggests that the hope of the recurrently depart-ing wanderer to be just once accompanied silently and mutely by the mulberry tree of life is never fulfilled. There was always new growth, insistent like the infant's longing scream, refusing to allow any peace and quiet.

Let us ask further who is addressed with the first You. Indeed, nothing more definite than what- or whoever next should welcome one after this summer of restless striding. Since a new scream of the thirst for life always accompanied the I, he is receptive to the contrast of the snow, that uniformity in which there is no longer any temptation or appeal. But this is precisely what a welcome should be, that is, the promise of a reception.

----

*In German, both *Maul* and *Mund* are equivalent to the English "mouth." The two words have distinct connotations, the former being rather perjorative (as in "shut your mouth"); moreover, *Beere* and *Blume* are used in expres-sions that refer to rhetorical flourish, again with different connotations (the former being again rather perjorative). Gadamer's insistence on following the proper transpositional movement involves a recognition of the quali-tative difference between poetic purity and the braggard's garishness.

**The German term here "sich einkehren" refers both to self-communion and to putting up at an inn.

Who can define what is at play here between desire and renunciation, between summer and winter, life and death, scream and stillness, word and silence? These verses express a readiness to accept what comes next, whatever it may be. Thus it seems to me completely possible to read this readiness ultimately as the readiness for death, that is, as the acceptance of the last, most extreme antithesis to too much life. The theme of death is constantly present in Celan, even in this cycle. At the same time, it is necessary to recall the special contextual function of this poem as proem to a cycle entitled "Breath-crystal." The title points to the sphere of breath and thus to the event of language formed by it.

So we ask again: what does snow mean here? Is it the experience *[Erfahrung]* of writing poetry which is alluded to here? Is it perhaps the word of the poem itself which is pronounced here, inasmuch as this word, in its discretion, preserves the wintery stillness that has been offered like a gift? Or does it refer to all of us and the dumbness that comes after too many words, that dumbness we all know and which can appear to all of us as true charity? The question cannot be answered. It is futile to differentiate between me and you, between the I of the poet and all of us whom the poem reaches. The poem says to the poet, as well as to all of us, that the stillness is welcome. It is the same stillness heard in the turn of breath, the ever so quiet recurrence of the act of breathing. More than anything, this is the 'breath-turn,' the sensuous experience of the silent, calm moment between inhaling and exhaling. I do not want to deny that Celan does not only associate this moment of turning breath, this instant when breath returns, with calm self-restraint, but that he also allows the subdued hope bound up with every return *[Umkehr]* to resonate. As he says in "Meridian": "Poetry: that can mean a breath-turn." But one ought not thereby diminish the meaning of the "quiet" breath which predominates in this sequence. This poem is a genuine proem, and as in musical composition, it establishes the key for the whole with the very first tone. The poems in this sequence are, in fact, as quiet and barely perceptible as the breath-turn. They offer witness to a last constriction of life and, simultaneoulsy, represent anew its recurring resolution, or better, not its resolution, but its elevation to a secure linguistic form *[Sprachgestalt]*. One hears it the way one hears the deep stillness of winter that blankets everything. Something ever so quiet crystallizes, something ever so small, so light, and yet so precise: the true word.

CORRODED BY the undreamed,
the sleeplessly traveled bread-land
digs up the life-mountain.

From its soil
you knead anew our names,
with an eye
like yours
on each of my fingers,
I probe them for
a place, through which I
can wake onto you,
the bright
Hunger-candle in my mouth.

VON UNGETRÄUMTEM geätzt,
wirft das schlaflos durchwanderte Brotland
den Lebensberg auf.

Aus seiner Krume
knetest du neu unsre Namen,
die ich, ein deinem
gleichendes
Aug an jedem der Finger,
abtaste nach
einer Stelle, durch die ich
mich zu dir heranwachen kann,
die helle
Hungerkerze im Mund.

A mole is active. That this is evoked by a primary semantic datum should not be disputed. The verb "digs up" is unambiguous. That the subject of this "digging up" is the bread-land need not be confusing, but simply initiates the first transposition: from the "mole" to the blind movement of life, which seems like a sleepless journey through the "bread-land." This evokes the work of earning one's bread, bread-winning and everything implied by the mortgaging of one's life. The poem thus says: What drives this restlessly burrowing quality we call life is undreamed dream. It is thus something neglected or refused whose constant bite keeps driving further; it corrodes. Corrosive acids leaking out of something which is made harmful by its refusal: this is one of the key metaphors for the cycle we are considering, and indeed for human destiny as the poet sees it. The journey goes through the bread-land, which promises to make one full, but the journeying leads nowhere. This journeying and burrowing occur sleeplessly, which means there is no recuperation in sleep or dream, and so the hill is dug up more and more. It becomes an entire life-mountain. But here that sounds as if life is buried under its own burdensome weight. It leaves its traces, just as the mole reveals his tracks when he digs up a molehill.

In fact, with all of our accumulating experience, we are the life-mountain. This is shown in the continuation of the poem: "From its soil you knead anew our names." It is possible that certain biblical or Jewish-mystical associations are concealed here. Even if one doesn't recognize them, but simply hears the verse from Genesis while simultaneously leaving it behind, Celan's verse makes sense. If it is life's heavy load from which our names are kneaded anew, then it must be the whole of our experience of the world which is constructed out of this material of experience. In the poem this is called "our names." For the name is what is first given to us, and what we are not quite yet. In giving a name, one cannot be sure of what will become of the person one names. This is true of all names. Only in the course of life do they become what they are: just as we become what we are, so the world also becomes what it is for us. This implies that the "names" must be constantly kneaded anew, or

[handwritten margin notes: OUR NAMES; + one Becomes; why not / my mouth is a hungry candle, / My Tongue a hungry Candle]

at least they are understood to be in constant formation. By whom is not said. But it is a "You." The alliteration of "new" and "names" unites the second half of the verse in such a way that the accent of a slight hiatus falls in the middle, the effects of which continue into the next line. At this point what is common to all—our "names"—is suddenly isolated as an I: "which I . . ." With this sudden "I" the movement of life first acquires its own secret direction, inasmuch as the "I" reaches up against the constantly growing coverture and seeks a passage into the open. Not smothered under the growing life-mountain or life-hill being dug up here, the I is still active and in search of seeing and brightness—even if blind like the mole. With its probing hand, the "I" can only perceive what is closest. Yet that is still perception. Our blind eye is like "yours." Perhaps the poet is alluding to the mole's hand, those peculiarly formed smooth surfaces of the digging hand with which the mole digs the passages that will lead him in the darkness toward the brightness of an opening. In any case, there is a tension between digging in the darkness and striving for the light. But the path through the darkness is not only the path that leads to the brightness; it is itself a path of brightness, itself a being bright *[Hellsein]*. One notices how "brightness" really spreads out in the penultimate line by the fact that the attribute "bright" stands out by itself. It is a special brightness. For the activity of the I is at work here, and this is nothing more than waking (waking onto). But waking takes up the renunciation of sleep and dream brought up at the beginning, just as "hunger-candle" refers to hungering, that is, to the rejection of the filling bread which loads the life-mountain. This fixation on brightness and the drive for the brightness is thus like an act of fasting. The closing image of the "hunger-candle in my mouth" reveals this through a certain religious custom whereby what is sought after, the 'You,' is ritually revered. As I was told by Tschizewskij, in the Balkans there is a tradition of the hunger-candle, which makes pious fasting visible to everybody (by the door of the church)—a kind of prayer- and supplication- fast, performed by parents hoping for the return of a son. Analogously, it is a "fast" which accompanies the striving for brightness. But what is remarkable about this fast is apparently that the one striving for brightness holds the hunger-candle *in his mouth.* That should indeed suggest that this is not about fasting, but that the I renounces all the richly filling words to which one resigns oneself in life—in order to be prepared for the true, luminous word. The ritual thus speaks of another kind of an act of faith. Apparently, there is no ritual of the hunger-candle *in one's mouth*! With this paradoxical association, the poem inverts the evoked custom of fasting. It is a different fasting, and the reason why it is performed is also different. Milojcic tells me that he knows the tradition of the hunger-candle differently: whenever someone became impoverished and was prohibited from begging by his former social position, he would appear by the door of the church disguised with the "hunger-candle" in order to receive donations without looking or being seen. In this case the candle would not give notice of a voluntary fast, but of the misery of hunger. Either way the poem says "in my mouth"—it concerns the true word for which I hunger, or which I bring about through hunger *[herbeihungere].* This can also be surmised, I believe, without folkloric information if one simply considers the tension between the ritual hunger-candle and "in my mouth." Does the hunger-candle, like all candles, also suggest that the time for our hungering pursuit of the brightness is limited? Perhaps. Regardless: one does not stop striving for the brightness as long as one probes "the names." The movement of the poem is clearly two-fold. All people undergo the first movement inasmuch as they are driven by undreamed dreams which mark a longer and longer trail of life and dig up a mountain that grows more and more burdensome. The other movement is the subterranean movement of the "I," which presses on like a blind mole into the brightness. One recalls Jacob Burckhardt: "The spirit is a burrower."

Let us follow once more the movement of transposition which we have come upon: Who is "you" here? The one who kneads the names anew, who has an eye that truly sees, who promises true satiety and illumination? Who is I and who is you? The transition to the I is sudden and sharply accentuated. It is raised up out of the fate common to all. Everyone's life-mountain is dug up constantly, and from it the meaning and meaninglessness of

every single life is formed. In this way, all of our "names" are
kneaded. And yet not everyone: only one I, which is "I" here,
probes these names. This suggests the activity of the poet, who
attempts it with names—with all names. This confirms that
"name" does not only mean people's names. It clearly means
the entire mountain of words; it means language, which is
deposited over the entire experience of life like a covering
burden. It is language which is probed, that is, tested for its
permeability, for the possibility of maybe somewhere permitting the breakthrough into brightness. This seems to me to
describe the destitution, as well as the distinction, of the poet.
But is it the poet's alone?

INTO THE GROOVES
of heaven's coin in the door-crack
you press the word,
from which I unrolled,
when with trembling fists
I dismantled the roof over us,
slate by slate,
syllable by syllable,
for the sake of the copper-
shimmer of the beggar's-
pan up there.

IN DIE RILLEN
der Himmelsmünze im Türspalt
preßt du das Wort,
dem ich entrollte,
als ich mit bebenden Fäusten
das Dach über uns
abtrug, Schiefer um Schiefer,
Silbe um Silbe, dem Kupfer-
schimmer der Bettel-
schale dort oben
zulieb.

These are bitter lines. In the published editions one reads "heaven's acid" instead of "heaven's coin." That should be corrected. But the question remains how the version of the published editions could have been understood—that it was understandable, at least to some extent, can hardly be doubted. It is supported not only by the poet's own bearing, since he reportedly remained quite calm after taking note of the printed mistake, but the coherence of meaning of the whole is generally strong enough to allow for the interchangeability of individual elements. This is what Walter Benjamin described with the concept of *das Gedichtete**. And if this were not the case, then all interpretation, which must work with uncertain conjectures, would be without value. We will consider both versions together in order to situate each of them within the whole of the poem.

Between the corrosive bite of heaven's acid, from which we are apparently separated by a never-to-be-opened door and which we would not be able to endure anyway, and the coppered beggar's pan "up there," spans the arch of a single sentence. In essence, this is a theology of a self-withholding heaven. Yet the door is pervious. The heaven's acid, from which we are blocked by the door, has eaten away grooves in the crack of the door, allowing something to come through. What comes through is the word. The metaphor of the corrosive acid is clearly applied to heaven because it withholds itself. Its consuming bite derives from its self-withholding—and yet we seek every drop of what reaches us—namely, the word.

Nevertheless, one must acknowledge that the text says "heaven's coin," not "heaven's acid." The conception of the image is thus utterly different. The genitive of "heaven's coin" is no longer attributed objectively to "grooves," but understood as a subjective genitive: the coin has grooves. There is no answer to the question of how the coin comes through the door-crack. That it is stuck there suffices. One imagines that it might be used

---

*The term comes from Benjamin's early essay, "Zwei Gedichte von Friedrich Hölderlin," and might be translated approximately as "the poeticized," or "poetic ground." See Benjamin's *Gesammelte Schriften*, Band II (Frankfurt: Suhrkamp Verlag, 1983), p. 105.

to open the door, but the door does not open; it provides no real entry. Instead, something forces its way out through the door. The grooves of the coin apparently make the door pervious. This slight permeability appears to depend not on the coin itself, the legitimate entry fee for heaven (or the exit- and access-fee from heaven?), but rather something which is on the coin, and indeed, which points to a blank and newly minted coinage without having anything to do with the coin's worth. This is quite obscure. Is it an elaborate symbol for grace? In any case, the attempt to defray the entry fee failed. All that we have from this self-withholding heaven is the word. Is that what is meant? Something so Lutheran?

What is certain is that the heaven's coin corresponds to the "beggar's pan up there." Both are associated with an unattainable Beyond. In the pan, coins are collected (coins from heaven? coins for heaven?), and it is this pathetic treasure toward which it appears the man is striving who infers his calling [Bestimmung] from the "word," the only one we have from the whole of heaven's fortune.

These are indeed bitter lines, no matter which version is taken as a basis. Yet it is clear that nothing can be disclosed about heaven except what you—once again this unknown You— force through the porousness of the obstructing door. This is not a flowing message of salvation, but rather a painstakingly extorted word; moreover, the effort seems strangely inverted. For apparently it is not we who are struggling to come in or out, but the word which supposedly wants out. That's how the You wants it. Does that mean that we are obstructing the truth, and that the truth is not at all withheld from us? Is it we who, so to speak, keep the door closed, or can't find the key, because we believe in the value of our coins? I raise all of these questions with the awareness that, in any case, what is evoked is a theology of the *Deus absconditus*.

One other difficulty: once the word is out and present, it is I who unrolled from it. Who is "I"? Am "I" from the word? Am I the word in the same way that every creature is a word of creation? The word to which I seek to return now and ever after—is that the word from which I come? This would make sense with the most extreme estrangement from God. For we all live under the roof of language. Perhaps it is true for all of us that we each would prefer to dismantle the roof which offers us common protection by taking away the portal and prospect, in order to look into the open. Certainly more than anyone the poet says of himself here something that is perhaps true for everyone. The covering of words is like a roof over us. They secure the familiar. But insofar as they envelope us completely with familiarity, they inhibit any view of the unfamiliar. Syllable by syllable, that is, laboriously and tirelessly, the poet—or is it each of us?— seeks to dismantle what is covering. This "syllable by syllable" dismantling seems to correspond to what we encountered in the previous poem as the probing of names and the waking onto. Both poems appear to describe a desperate effort to strive for the brightness above.

But does one ever reach the goal? The poem's answer is shattering. At best, what was attained here through the work of the trembling fists may be in truth nothing more than the copper beggar's pan, with its otherworldly shimmer. That a completely normal beggar's pan on a Paris street inspired the poet, as Bollack told me, does not change the fact that the poem speaks of a "beggar's pan up there" and thus demands a certain transposition from us. The poem transposes the beggar's pan into the context of piety and the desire for salvation. But with what tone? Expectation? Hardly. More like this: with our idea of salvation we can reach no further than this beggar's pan in which the offerings are collected—the most profane of all Church implements. Or this: we reach only the meagre benevolence of a "collection," in which there is neither warmth nor love. Either way, nothing genuinely sacred awaits me when I seek to dismantle the protective roof. It is scarcely even the reflection of the sacred. Or perhaps it isn't even sacred, but something whose false shimmer only gleams like the sacred? Either way, the one who desperately makes the effort is full of bitterness and aware of the disappointment that awaits him.

But let us leave all theology aside and examine the individual phrases. What does it mean that "I" unrolled from the word? The use of the term "unroll," as well as the "syllable by syllable" dismantling, at first suggests the activity of unrolling a scroll and deciphering an ancient text, which might be the poetic *the word from which I myself / unroll.*

word. But the word "unrolled" is used here intransitively. "I" unrolled from the word that has seeped through from above, from that tiniest drop of an otherworldy, heavenly substance. That sounds paradoxical. It is not "I" who rolls out the word-syllable by syllable—like a scroll—rather, it is the word from which I myself unroll. Thus it seems that the poet himself comes from the word and that his whole effort is geared toward reattaining this word from which he comes and which he knows to be his. No doubt this breathlessly desperate search for the word is intended not just for any word and syllable, but for the true Word, the Word which contains him who seeks it. It thus appears to be the poet who refers to himself as "I" here, and who lives completely in the word. For the task of the poet is to seek the true word, not the word which comes from the usual, protective roof of every day, but the one which arrives from beyond as if it were his true home. Therefore, the poet must dismantle the scaffolding of every day words syllable by syllable. He must fight against the ordinary, customary, obscuring, and levelling function of language in order to lay open a view of the glimmer above. That is poetry.

But there is something else in this. Indeed it says that the poet unrolls from the word in his poetry when, word by word, he looks up at his origin in the true word—and yet perceives in the sacred nothing more than its most profane and pathetic shimmer, perhaps only a false gleam distorted by begging. As a result, the unrolling takes on another, negative tone: with the dismantling of the roof, the search for the right words ("when I dismantled"), the poet does not return home, he loses himself. He "unrolls" from the word which he actually is; he is hopelessly separated from it, and toils in vain—with trembling fists—to return to it. "We translate, without having the original text" (G[ünter] Eich). Once again, one asks oneself: is it really only the poet for whom the real word remains unattainable, even though it belongs to him? Or is it not rather the experience of all of us to be separated from the real word and its truth precisely insofar as we make words and actively—"with trembling fists"—go after something which we would like to have, but which is unattainable, and which, in the end, does not even repay the effort?

see how to make an elephant

IN THE STREAMS north of the future
I cast the net, which you
hesitantly load
with stone-written
shadows.

[handwritten margin note: with shadows inscribed on stones?]

IN DEN FLÜSSEN nördlich der Zukunft
werf ich das Netz aus, das du
zögernd beschwerst
mit von Steinen geschriebenen
Schatten.

One must not only read the poem precisely with regard to its line breaks, one must also hear it that way. Celan's poems, which usually have short lines, are very precise in that regard. In more broadly flowing verses, as in the *Duino Elegies*, which, especially in the printings that followed the first edition, could not avoid a great number of mechanical line breaks, only very distinct verse caesuras have the signatory conciseness of the concluding lines of these Celan poems. In this example, the concluding verse is a single word: "shadows"—a word that falls as heavily as what it signifies. Yet, it is a conclusion, and as such, it draws together the proportions of the whole. Moreover, complementing the evoked meaning, "shadows fall" always means that they are cast. Where shadows fall and darken there is always light and radiance, and indeed it does get bright in this poem. What is evoked is the clarity and coldness of nearly frozen water. The sun shines through the water to the very bottom. The stones which load down the nets cast the shadows. All this is highly sensuous and concrete: a fisherman casts the net, and someone else helps him by loading it down. Who am I? And who are you? The I is a fisherman who casts the net. Casting the net is an act of pure expectation. Whoever casts the net has done everything he can do, and he must wait and see if something is caught. It is not said when this act is completed. It is a kind of gnomic present; in other words, it occurs again and again. This

[handwritten margin note: gnomic present]

is underscored by the plural "in the streams," which, unlike the closely related "waters," does not refer to an indefinite location, but rather to very specific places sought out because they promise a good catch. These places all lie "north of the future," that is, they lie much farther away, beyond the usual paths and courses, out where no one else fishes. This is apparently a statement about an I with very special expectations. It expects what is to come at a point where no expectation from experience extends. But doesn't every I have such expectations? Is there not something in every I which reaches out into a future that lies beyond what can be counted on in advance? This I, so different from the others, is precisely the I of any individual.

Now the artfully drawn arc of this poem, which consists of one simple sentence, rests on the fact that the I is not alone and cannot haul in the catch by itself. It needs the You. The You is situated emphatically at the end of the second line, as if at a standstill, like an indefinite question which will obtain meaning only in its continuation in the third verse, or rather in the second half of the poem. An activity is described here quite precisely. To load hesitantly does not mean an inner hesitation of indecisiveness or doubt which prevents the You, whoever it may be, from fully sharing the confidence of the fisherman-I. It would be completely mistaken to attribute such a meaning to this hesitation. What is described, rather, is the loading down of the net. To load the net down one must put in neither too much nor too little: too much, and the net will sink; too little, and it will push upwards. As the fisherman says, the net must "stand." This is what accounts for the hesitation of loading down. To load the net one must place the stones carefully, one by one, as if on a scale pan, with which the weight of something is balanced. For it all depends on finding the correct point of balance. Whoever does this by loading down the net helps make the catch possible.

However, the sensuous concretion of the process is artfully elevated into the imaginary and spiritual. Already the first line, with its perceptually elusive assemblage "north of the future," compels one to understand the statement in its generality. The same function is carried out in the second half of the poem by the no less elusive assemblage of a loading down with shadows—shadows, no less, written from stones. If the expectation inherent in being human was at first visible in the sensuous gesture of the fisherman, now the meaning of what expectation is and makes possible is determined more narrowly. For it seems that what is shown here is the interplay between two actions: the casting out and the loading down of the net. There is a mysterious tension between them, and yet together they are a unified act which alone promises a catch. In fact, the catch depends on this mysterious opposition between loading and casting. It would be wrong to think that loading down inhibits a pure cast into the future, that it is a disturbance of pure expectation due to encumbering insight into what pulls downward. Rather, it is only this tension which bestows the certainty of a future onto the emptiness of expectation and the vanity of hoping. The bold metaphor of the "written shadows" not only accentuates what is imaginary and spiritual in the act as a whole, it attests to something like sense. What is written can be deciphered. It means something, and isn't simply the dull resistance of the burdensome. Perhaps one can translate it like this: just as the act of the fisherman is promising only because of the interplay between casting and loading, so the sense in which human life is lived for the sake of the future does not represent merely an indefinite openness toward whatever comes, but is determined by what was, and how it has been preserved, as in a book written out of experiences and disappointments. *But who is this you?*

But who is this You? It almost sounds as if someone here knows just how much the I can be loaded, just how much the aspiring heart of human beings can endure without permitting hope to recede. An indefinite you—perhaps realized in the You of someone close by or far away, or even in the You that I myself am when I make the limits of reality perceptible to my own optimism. Either way, what is really present in these verses, and what lends reality to the I, is the interplay between I and You that promises a catch.

But then what is catch supposed to mean here? The fluid exchange between the poet and I allows us to understand it in both a particular and a general sense, or better yet: to recognize the general in the particular. The catch, which shall succeed, might be the poem itself. The poet might thus be referring to himself in saying that he casts the net out where clarity and calm find the waters of language limpid and permit him to expect that his extraordinary and unprecedented boldness will yield him a

[handwritten margin notes: See Stefan GEORGE / the mirror / the word]

[handwritten left margin: when the reader (or listener) enters & is permitted / to be "I" the good imaginative / ???]

catch. That the poet means himself when he represents himself in this way as an I that fishes can also be supported by context—not only the larger context of world literature, which loves to seize poetic treasure out of the dark depths of a fountain or a sea; one thinks, for example, of Stefan George's famous poems "The Mirror" and "The Word." But it is also supported by the particular context of this poem cycle, which sets off the true poem, that which is no "false poem" *[Meingedicht]*, no misleading oath of presumption, against the vain production of words wherein language is wrenched back and forth. It is thus completely justified to understand this poem in terms of the poet and his expectation of finding the right word. And yet what is described here goes far beyond the particularity of the poet. And not only here. One of the fundamental metaphors of the modern age is the poet's activity as a paradigm for human existence itself. The right word, immortalized by the poet, is not his special artistic achievement, but more generally, a symbol of the possibilities of human experience, one that permits the reader to be the I, that is, the poet. In our verses, I and You are described in terms of a mysterious solidarity of achievement which is not only between the poet and his genius or God. This being, human or God, does not load down by piling on word shadows which restrict freedom. In this poem, which may very well be taken to mean the unique achievement of poetic existence, the identity of the I is expressed only insofar as it becomes clear who You is. If the poet's verses make this commonality concrete, then each of us occupies precisely the position which the poet claims as his own. Who am I and who are you? The poem provides its own answer to this question by keeping it open.

O[tto] Pöggeler suggests that "north of the future" be understood as a landscape of death, since any future coming toward us is overtaken by the "intangible abyss" of death—a radicalization of basic human experience which would make it necessary to understand the You as the thought of death that weighs upon all existence. It is true that in this way "north of the future" would be understood more precisely: the point at which there is no longer any future, and thus, simultaneously, no longer any expectation. And yet: a haul of fish. This is worth pondering further. Is it the acceptance of death which promises the new catch?

BEFORE YOUR LATE FACE,
single-
handedly between
nights also transforming me,
something came to stand,
which was with us once before, un-
touched by thoughts.

VOR DEIN SPÄTES GESICHT,
allein-
gängerisch zwischen
auch mich verwandelnden Nächten,
kam etwas zu stehn,
das schon einmal bei uns war, un-
berührt von Gedanken.

For a long time, this poem seemed especially difficult to me, for the unambiguousness of what it states presents an especially wide scope for interpretation. Is it a love poem? Does it speak of human being and God? Are they nights of love which have transformed "me," or nights of loneliness?

As is often the case with short-lined poems, the brevity and precision of its composition places great weight on the last verse. "Touched by thoughts" is almost like an epigrammatic seal. The whole basically must be understood from here. The tension-laden separation in "un-/touched by thoughts" isolates the aspect of being touched by thought. But in what sense? There are two possible ways of understanding it: as a positive statement, strengthened by the line break, about the untouchedness of what came before "your face," namely, that it is nothing expressly known or thought. Or, as a statement about the fact that what "was with us once before" is different now, namely that it is "touched by thoughts," and thereby transformed. It certainly does not mean "untouched before and after." The statement of the poem is completely controlled by the tension between "before" and "after." It speaks of a "late" face, implying an earlier one; it speaks of a "once before" and of "transforming" nights. The tension between Now and Then must thus also lie in "un-/touched," which contains a line break not without good reason.

The question here involves the most extreme peculiarities of rhythm, versification, and assemblage of meaning *[Sinnfügung]*. It is a question of the ultimate coherence of meaning—and this seems to me to speak for the interpretation I've suggested, that a new consciousness has arrived. For that "something" which comes to stand here would remain much too indefinite if nothing were being said about it. Even if it means that the untouchedness of thoughts is destroyed by thinking, one still understands that "something" has arrived, namely, with all its indeterminateness, a new awareness that embraces aloneness. Growing awareness, distance, aloneness—this is not the disappointed realization of lost accessibility, a kind of alienation. Quite the contrary, what occurs here is mutual recognition: the nights are referred to as "also transforming me"—meaning they also transform you. The distance now perceived had always been there in what is termed "discretion," including that "infinite discretion," which is how Rilke described his relationship to God.*

The actual experience expressed by these verses is this: since then it has become otherwise. What had been untouched by thoughts is so no longer, once and for all time. The conclusiveness of what has arrived is pronounced in the epigrammatic last line "touched by thoughts."

Here the question of who I and You are now appears pivotal. But even here one must not ask the question in this way. What matters is that between the I that speaks here and the You to whom it speaks, the story of a close relationship is recalled, the beginning of which lies further back. This is suggested by the adjective "late," which is attributed to the face; moreover, it sounds as if in the meantime this face has withdrawn into itself and closed itself off more severely. For it says "single-handedly," which means not only going it alone, but also consciously choosing to be and remain alone. Once again, it is the division of the word that concretizes this tension of being alone. It suggests

---

*See Rilke's letter to Ilse Jahr of February 22, 1923.

both being alone and the will to be so. This is confirmed from another perspective by "my" admission that I have also been transformed. What has arrived here "before your late face" should not be taken, however, as something alien that had not been there before. For it was already once "with us." What has since changed does not completely negate the intimacy of a mutual relationship. It is not something alien. But one should not ask what it is. Even the speaker does not seem to know how to name it. It is "nothing."

The only hint that the poem offers is contained in the phrase "un-touched by thoughts." It implies that in the meantime one has had thoughts, and that through these thoughts something has come to stand. One notices that it does not say: something came in between. This is not some special event that changed everything, but rather the result of time itself, which reveals nothing new, but simply allows something that is familiar because it was once with us to stand for itself. It says "with us" and not "between us." What comes to consciousness here is perhaps nothing other than aloneness in reciprocal intimacy.

It thus appears scarcely necessary to know who I and You are. For the poem speaks about something that happens to both. I and you are both transformed, self-transforming. What happens to them is time. Whether this You bears the face of a neighbor, or is the Wholly Other of the divine, the message is that with all the intimacy they share, they become increasingly aware of the distance remaining between them. In those nights, that is, in the closeness and warmth of being together—which can extinguish everything else and resolve whatever divides—right there something was transformed and something came to stand. Is it in any way divisive? It arrived "before your" face. This certainly suggests that I no longer have such direct access to "you," yet also that I am not separated from "you." It was, after all, already "with us." It seems more as if with the new knowledge, the distance that had always been there were being affirmed, the distance of the hidden God, or the remoteness of the one nearest to us.

THROUGH THE MELANCHOLY RAPIDS
on past the blank
wound-mirror:
there the forty
decorticated life-trees are floated.

The only anti-
swimmer, you
count them, touch them
all.

DIE SCHWERMUTSSCHNELLEN HINDURCH
am blanken
Wundenspiegel vorbei:
da werden die vierzig
entrindeten Lebensbäume geflößt.

Einzige Gegen-
schwimmerin, du
zählst sie, berührst sie
alle.

    This is about the experience of time. At one point the allu-
sion in the poem becomes tangible. Someone is thinking about
being forty years old. Of course: the poet. Certainly. And yet what
the poet says here about himself contains something general,
something so common to us all that these particular forty years are
not the poet's alone. In speaking the lyrical word, the "I" that
includes us all is so present that "I" is not even mentioned in the
entire poem. This "I" that includes us all thinks about its forty
years, that is, it thinks about all that has come upon it, as well as
all that it has come upon: times of melancholy, river rapids, which
are dangerous not because of their existence, but because they
appear suddenly and unpredictably. The dangerousness of something that suddenly comes over one is evoked by the single word
"melancholy-rapids"—as is the fact that "I" came through all its
trials. Now it goes through stiller waters, on past the mirroring sea,
whose surface, in contrast to the river rapids, is so stationary that
it reflects everything. In it there is thus knowledge and recollec-

tion. It reflects the visible traces of visible injuries, wounds which become painfully evident to life as it rushes away. Most of all, it is these wounds which arise in the balance of life.

And yet the actual movement in the poem is that life goes on, past the bitter disappointments and the transparency of naked suffering. The life-trees of the years drifting away here are "decorticated." This might mean either that the core is exposed (for the person remembering?) such that everything inessential is stripped away, or perhaps that what is actually living is no longer present. Decorticating prevents the sap-stream of life from continuing to rise and fall. All that remains is its wooden core. In any case: the life-trees are floated. The force of the water carries them away, downstream. Against this stream of expiration [Vergehen] someone swims for whom, as the only anti-swimmer, these differences of sudden disappointments, this mirroring clarity of wounds, indeed everything they include in life, does not appear to exist at all. This anti-swimmer is addressed as "You," admiringly, approvingly.

The last line "all" makes the comprehensiveness of this anti-movement clear. The anti-swimmer numbers and touches all these life-trees. The uniformity and the unerring precision at work here make it certain, it seems to me, that the anti-swimmer is time itself passing by. Nothing can remain as constant, steady, and inseparable from the first year of life on—not human remembering, memory, nor even the compassionate concern of others. Plato taught that time is number, counted movement [bewegte Außereinander].* The counter-swimmer here is obviously more than simply some standard with which to measure movement. She does something by resisting the displacing current of expiration.** Only in that way is she like a constant standard, summing up and measuring everything; by counting, she can be sure of all that flows by, as if touching it by hand. In this way nothing is excluded; everything belongs, including the "uncounted" sufferings left behind and forgotten in "life." What is counted is thus the entire sum of lived time. Now, Aristotle

*See Gadamer's essay, "Idea and Reality in Plato's *Timaeus*," in *Dialogue and Dialectic: Eight Hermeneutical Studies on Plato*, trans. P. Christopher Smith (New Haven: Yale University Press, 1980), pp. 156–93.

**The word Celan uses for "counter-swimmer" is *Gegenschwimmerin*, like the word for "time" *(Zeit)*, a feminine form in German.

[handwritten annotations: "ARISTOTLE — the soul is present along with time — / the soul is a function the create time"]

taught that the soul is present somehow along with time. The counter-force which does not allow itself to be swept along and does not cease to be there and to count everything is thus not time itself, but rather the Self that stands and withstands, the Self that "I" am, and wherein time is constituted. As Augustine showed, in the Self one's life history comes together as a whole. In the Self, time is first present. There is something mysterious in the self-sameness of the I. It lives because it forgets—but it also lives as I only because all its days have been counted "for it" and are counted, unforgettable. It is the essence of time that nothing of what I was is left out. But certainly no forty year old, or for that matter, anybody looking back, is actually conscious of grasping anything in that way. The I experiences here precisely this difference between time, which counts everything, and its own consciousness of life. With such harmony of time, and with the serenity of a consciousness that can imagine time for itself, the forty year old becomes aware of his own higher Self.

❖ ❖ ❖

THE NUMBERS, allied
with the doom of images
and anti-
doom.

Set on top of it the
skull, on whose
sleepless temples a mad-
dening hammer,
sings this all to the
world-beat.

DIE ZAHLEN, im Bund
mit der Bilder Verhängnis
und Gegen-
verhängnis.

Der drübergestülpte
Schädel, an dessen
schlafloser Schläfe ein irr-
lichternder Hammer
all das im Welttakt
besingt.

Here, too, the poem is about the experience of time. "The numbers" takes up the counting of time. Time appears here as doom, because it stands in league with the "doom and anti-doom" of images. "The doom of images" apparently refers to what is awake behind the skull, the unavoidable doom of consciousness in which something is always pictured. Something neither wished, nor summoned must be there. The numbers, this sequence of moments, is not for itself. Because they are "allied," they always also insure that images are present as elements of inner experience [Erfahrung]. Thus these images inextricably coinciding with numbers and time are, like time, not only a "doom," that is, a necessary, unalterable occurrence. They also function as an "anti-doom." This suggests that they also oppose the numbers, oppose the monotony of the sequence which pounds unceasingly like a hammer. Yet these images are also themselves a doom. In relation to the images, the word "doom" thus acquires a new anti-meaning, namely that it conceals something, such that the concealed is no longer visible, no longer displayed in its actual form.* Insofar as the anti-doom of the images is at the same time both the concealed and the concealing, doom also acquires the double meaning of being simultaneously concealed and concealing. The images are both concealed and concealing in relation to the numbers, time, and unrelenting expiration. As in "allied with images," this is not only an incessant pounding of ephemerality, but also a veil that lies over the present; in order to forget it, another veil is lowered, the colorful tapestry of images.

Time is the inner sense in which the succession of ideas [Vorstellungen] is found. Kant has taught us this, as well as Aristotle, if only in a preliminary way. What is strange is that the endlessness of this sequence and images is enclosed under a sort of helmet: the skull, upon whose wall of externality this inner endlessness is manifest in the hammer's beating of a time pulse. Now, the poem says "sings to the world-beat." It is clear that the time-hammer's beat is the world-beat; it encompasses everything. But what does it mean that the pounding hammer "sings" this entire inner sequence? Obviously no music is made from this

---

*Gadamer draws here on the etymological relation of *Verhängnis* ("doom") to the verb *verhängen* ("conceal").

beat of incessant passing. The bold metaphor "sings" forms a concluding verse and thereby obtains a powerful stress, the emphasis of paradox, which avows and disavows itself. At any rate "sings" means: not to oppose, but to praise, and in this praising, to make present. What does that mean? How is it that the maddening hammer, the convulsion of consciousness that only follows and goes along with the stream of time and image, can also say "yes" to it and make it completely mine—as the "I think" that must be able to accompany all of my ideas?

Or is it precisely the monotony of the hammer's beat of ephemerality which, in a bitter oxymoron, is named "singing"? The semantic datum still seems unambiguous to me: in the great beat of time, which is like a pulse beating, the flaring up of consciousness is like an anti-doom. The changing content of images maddeningly enlivens the monotony of the unceasing sequence. That a word-play lurks nearby—as is generally the case with Celan—is shown in the second stanza by the phrase "sleepless temple."* Like all word-play, it embodies a breach in thought, or better, a hidden harmony, which, as Heraclitus knew, is stronger than an open one. In fact, it is the mystery of consciousness itself, insofar as it can be sleep and sleeplessness in one, a sleeplessness in sleep. One is awake when one is conscious of oneself. But one who is conscious of himself in this way is always like someone who has just awakened from sleep. So sure are we of our self-sameness in our self-consciousness, that being awake can without question encompass sleep, faint recollection, and forgetting. Now, is the hammer that pounds on the temples in the monotony of an unrelenting continuation of time, song?—or is it song-like? Either way, it means something which comes into being and to a standstill. This is the real message. The monotony is broken because the hammer not only beats the world-beat, but sings to the beat everything that emerges in the utter palpability of images. The changing images enter into a constant being that resists the expiration into silence, a constant being in which agreement occurs.

---

*Celan's verse reads "schlafloser Schläfe." The root of the German verb for "sleep" (*schlafen*) is thus contained in the word for "temples" (*Schläfe*).

PATHS IN THE SHADOW-ROCK
of your hand

Out of the four-finger-furrow
I grub for myself the
petrified blessing.

WEGE IM SCHATTEN-GEBRÄCH
deiner Hand.

Aus der Vier-Finger-Furche
wühl ich mir den
versteinerten Segen.

Following hermeneutical principle, I begin with the emphatic concluding verse. For it contains the core of this short poem. It speaks of "petrified blessing." Blessing is no longer granted openly and flowingly. The closeness and charity of the benefactor is foregone to such an extent that blessing is present only in petrifaction. Now, the poem says: This blessing of the benefactory hand is sought after with the grubbing and despairing fervor of an indigent. Accordingly, the benefacting hand is inverted boldly into the hand where palm-reading can reveal a message of beneficent hope. The context tells us what "shadow-rock" means. When the hand is clenched a little and the creases cast shadows, then, in the crumbly "rock" of the hand, that is, in the lattice of folds and gaps, the breaks interpreted by the palm-reader become visible. The palm-reader reads from them the language of destiny or of character. The "four-finger-furrow" is thus the continuous transverse crease which, without the thumb, comprises the four fingers into a unity.

How strange all this is! The I, be it the poet or we ourselves, seeks to "grub" out of the hand of benefaction a blessing that has become distant and ungraspable. But this cannot occur if one simply trusts the skillful deciphering of a mysterious play of lines. In truth, the palm-reader's situation clearly invoked here is fundamentally contrastive. One must admit that palm-reading possesses a peculiar attraction when it is performed seriously rather than for simple amusement. The undiscloseability of the future imbues any message about such signs with a sense of seductive mystery. But here it is quite different. The seeker's fervor and desperation is so great that he cannot simply dwell

half-seriously and half in jest on the skillful interpretation of the
hand's and the future's secret writing. Like a man about to die
of thirst, he seeks in the confusion of palm lines nothing less
than the greatest, deepest, and, in truth, least mysterious furrow
of all, in whose shadow nothing is written. But his need is so
great that from this no longer benefactory hand-furrow he still
implores something like a blessing.

Whose hand is it? It is difficult to see in this benefactory hand
that no longer blesses anything but the hand of the hidden God,
whose abundance of blessedness has become indiscernible, and
only accessible to us as if in petrifaction, be it in the reified cer-
emony of religion, or the reified power of human faith. But once
again the poem does not decide who "You" is. Its only message is
the urgent need of the person who seeks a blessing from "your"
hand, regardless of whose it is. What he finds is a "petrified" blessing. Is that still a blessing? An ultimate blessing? From your hand?

❖ ❖ ❖

GRAY-WHITE of ex-
cavated steep
feeling.

Landwards, the dune grass
scattered here wafts
sand patterns over
the smoke of fountain songs.

An ear, severed, listens.
An eye, cut into strips,
copes with it all.

WEISSGRAU aus-
geschachteten steilen
Gefühls.

Landeinwärts, hierher-
verwehrter Strandhafer bläst
Sandmuster über
den Rauch von Brunnengesängen.

Ein Ohr, abgetrennt, lauscht.
Ein Aug, in Streifen geschnitten,
wird all dem gerecht.

The vulgar images of the cut-off ear and the eye cut into strips give this poem its unique character. One must and should feel a kind of revulsion at these vulgarities, which challenge the reader to subdue them by understanding. But what is to be understood here? I think it is this: No ear open to the world's melodies, no all-encompassing view inebriated with the world's golden overflow, corresponds accurately to what is. Only a listening so intense that the ear seems severed, "wholly ear," and an eye that spies through the narrowest slit—this seems to be what "cut into strips" means—can still perceive what is. For knowledge ("Smoke of fountain songs") comes from only the smallest detail, from the scarcely audible and scarcely visible.

Yet with the strictest omissions, "all" is still there: the sea—for the poem says "landwards"; the chalk cliffs in the gray-white of broken ground; and then, further inland, away from the encroaching sea, something completely different, something human: smoke and fountains. The steep coast evokes loneliness, but also the outcropping, the laying bare of what is otherwise hidden. Here, however, this is rendered as a "steep feeling." (One recalls Rilke's "drossy petrified rage").* What has been laid bare reaches into the depths of feeling as if into an abyss. This is contained in the word "steep." But this is not anything like a source of feelings. Gray-white, without color and life, it stands rigid, exposed to storms like a quarry that has been "excavated."

What actually begins in the second stanza, which opens with "landwards"? What is found there, landwards, is something less than the gray-white break line of the loneliness between the two great elements sea and land. But "landwards" suggests something like an expectation, as if the barren loneliness of depleted, "excavated" feeling could be relieved by the resonating tones of humanness. Nevertheless, the image changes: one should hear songs rising like smoke out of various openings of the depths, out of fountains. "Smoke of fountain songs" awakens a number

---

*See Rilke's "Tenth Elegy" (stanza 4, line 6): "oder, aus allem Vulkan, schlackig versteinerten Zorn."

of associations. The smoking chimneys of people's homes, village fountains, human sounds, singing. Yet with all that, we are also not far from the desolation of the beach. The sand grain blows its sand patterns over everything. The bleakness and barrenness of the sand dunes creeping up the land, and their monotonous pattern, describe a world becoming uniform, in which nothing human is manifest any more, and in which the song of the fountains is almost drowned out. This song, this self-proclaiming of humanness in a world covered over with sand, remains audible only to the most intense listening; only in momentary gaps can the most exacting watch glimpse what is humanly ordered. The vulgar horror of the concluding ear and eye metaphors permits us to sense the oppressive indigence of the world, in which feeling can scarcely still accomplish anything.

WITH MASTS SUNG EARTHWARDS,
heaven's wrecks are sailing.

Into this wood-song
you firmly sink your teeth.

You are the song-firm
pennant.

MIT ERDWÄRTS GESUNGENEN MASTEN
fahren die Himmelwracks.

In dieses Holzlied
beißt du dich fest mit den Zähnen.

Du bist der liedfeste
Wimpel.

Three short stanzas depict the scene of a shipwreck, which from the start is transformed into something unreal. It is a shipwreck in heaven. Yet even there a shipwreck means what we always imagine it to mean in shipwreck metaphors, beginning perhaps with Caspar David Friedrich's famous painting of the shipwreck in the ice of the Baltic Sea: the shattering of all hopes. It is an old theme. Here, too, the poet conjures up shattered hopes. But as a shipwreck in heaven it has a completely different scope. The masts of the wreck point toward the earth and not above. One recalls a profound line from Celan's Meridian speech: "Whoever stands on his head sees heaven as an abyss beneath him.",

Yet one thing is clear: these masts are "sung." They are songs, but not the kind that consolingly refer to the "above" or the "beyond." One recalls the inversion in [Celan's] "Tenebrae": "Pray to us, Lord."* One no longer seeks help from heaven, but from earth. The ships are all wrecked, but the song is still sung. The song of life still resounds even if the masts now motion toward the earth. It is thus the poet who clamps down on this "wood song" with [his] "teeth," that is, with ultimate and extreme effort, in order to prevent himself from going under completely. It is the song which holds him above water. Hence, it's called a "wood-song." Just as a drowning person does not let go of a floating rescue plank as his last support, as if to bite into it with his teeth, so the I fastens onto the song. And in a complete reversal of the shattered reality, after the shipwreck of heaven and all its promises, the poet calls himself a "pennant." He holds fast onto the song mast, that is, he cannot be separated from it. Just as the banner of a sinking ship is last to tower up over the water, so the poet with his song is a last proclamation and promise of life, a last holding up of hope. Pointedly, he is called

---

*See Gadamer's discussion of the poem in "Meaning and Concealment of Meaning in Paul Celan," pp. 168–78 in this volume.

"song-firm." For only the song will endure, not go under—one holds fast onto it after the shipwreck of all hopes directed toward heaven.

In this way, the poet speaks here of his work. But like the metaphor of the "song of life," which the reader takes here to mean life itself, so the "song-firm pennant" must mean not only the poet and his perseverance in hoping, but also the ultimate hoping of all creatures. Once again, there is no boundary between the poet and the human being, who holds up hope with every last bit of strength.

❖ ❖ ❖

TEMPLE-FORCEPS,
eyed by your jugal bone.
Its glint of silver there,
where it bit down:
you and the remainder of your sleep —
soon
it will be your birthday.

SCHLÄFENZANGE,
von deinem Jochbein beäugt.
Ihr Silberglanz da,
wo sie sich festbiß:
du und der Rest deines Schlafs —
bald
habt ihr Geburtstag.

This is clearly about the poet's response to the call of old age. The "temple-forceps" refers to the graying temples, a sign of encroaching age, gripping unrelentingly like a forceps. The second verse, "eyed by your jugal bone," nearly comes across as clinically anatomical, and yet "eyed" introduces a tone of watch-ful anxiety. As the poem continues, it becomes clear how think-ing about death gains intensity. For it says: "you and the remainder of your sleep"—a bold oxymoron indeed since it stands for the remainder of a life. And what does the pointed phrase "soon it will be your birthday" mean? It obviously does not mean: soon you will be born. Having a birthday does not mean being born; it is the recurring celebration of having been born. And for someone whose temples are already graying, the return of a birthday means an increased awareness of life's declivity and brevity. Nevertheless one does not actually detect in these verses a plaintive tone.

One would like to know who is actually being addressed here. Is the I speaking to itself? But it seems strange that "you and the remainder of your sleep" is comprised by a second person plural that celebrates a birthday together. One must begin to interpret at the point where the poem sounds peculiar, namely, with this ending. The ending conceals two antitheses: the first is an antithesis between the You that addresses itself and stays on the lookout, and the sleep which, following Heraclitus, Pindar, Euripides, Calderon, and many others, is another name for life. The second antithesis is contained in the contradiction between the expectant and joyful birthday celebration, and the premoni-tion of old age and death. The joy of expectation is heightened by the one-word verse "soon," and it turns into the speaker's abandonment of expectation as he becomes aware of aging. The joy of expectation is thus reversed into two antitheses of bitter-ness, a wonderful example of how ironic reversal, and the radi-ant intangibility that belongs to it, is elevated to poetic manifestation. For what sort of a birthday is this? What is cel-ebrated and commemorated here? The day of existential joyous-ness (as Count Yorck von Wartenburg once called the birthday)? But whose existence? To hear it correctly one must understand it this way: the existence of those who know themselves, accept themselves, and are fully aware of their own finitude. To be mature is everything.

IN THE HAILSTONE, in the
blighted corn-
cob, at home, obeying
the late, the hard
November stars:

in your heart-thread the
conversations of worms are knit—:

a string, from which
your arrow-writing whirs,
Archer.

BEIM HAGELKORN, im
brandigen Mais-
kolben, daheim,
den späten, den harten
Novembersternen gehorsam:

in den Herzfaden die
Gespräche der Würmer geknüpft—:

eine Sehne, von der
deine Pfeilschrift schwirrt,
Schütze.

   Just as the previous poem concerned the awareness of
thinking about death, this poem is also explicitly about death.
Undoubtedly the last word "Archer" is a metaphor for death. But
many other things also plainly allude to this sphere: the "hailstone," the "corn-cob" which has become "blighted," "late November." Celan comes from the East, and one feels how this
slow onset of the arduous eastern winter awakens in him knowledge of the ephemerality of existence, knowledge deeply inter-
woven with his feeling of life: thoughts of death, the conversations
of worms, are "knit into your heart-thread." It is like an inner

gnawing, or better, a most intimately understood certainty of the finitude and ephemerality of our existence.

The composition as a whole is unambiguously concise. There are two colons. The second is intensified by a hyphen. They allow the phrase at the end of the poem to follow like a conclusion after two premises. This concluding phrase comprises everything that has come before it in the image of a drawn bowstring from which the arrow whirs. But it isn't the arrow, death itself, which flies away from the bowstring, but the "arrow-writing." If the arrow is writing, it is a message, a proclamation. Doubtless this writing tells us something specific: it is the message of ephemerality that speaks from everything named in the poem. But it is a message. Therefore, the semantic elements of the text of the poem that must be distinguished as sustentative are those not only proclaiming ephemerality, but also decisively accepting the message of ephemerality. One sustentative occurrence of meaning is thus the word "obeying," which recognizes the setting in of winter. The corresponding "at home," in the hailstorm, in the blighted corn-cob, is similarly understood. Of course, "at home" does not refer literally to the actual eastern homeland, but to being at home in the heralds of winter, death, and ephemerality. Thus, the middle part of the poem contains a double affirmation. The signs of the coming winter and the heart's innermost certainty of death are affirmed. That is why the "conversations of worms" are "knitted into the heart-thread." The inner gnawing of ephemerality does not remain a being-gnawed-at from the outside; it is, rather, taken up completely inside. In that way, the two premises from which the conclusion is drawn are secured through affirmation. The conclusion is valid: the arrow that sends its message is the certainty of death, which never misses its mark. But there is more to it: the Archer Death writes his word into one single, great readiness.

Perhaps one ought to go a step further and also recognize the heart-thread as the bowstring from which the arrow-writing is shot. For the heart-thread, upon which the worms are gnaw-.ing, is in a certain way the resiliency of life itself—therein are knit the conversations of the worms. The concluding sentence deduces nothing new; it simply summarizes. The deep inner

certainty of ephemerality and death is not like the string of a
deadly bow, whose shot suddenly tears one apart; quite the
contrary, it is what life itself draws. It is not so much death that
comes from this string of the heart as it is the trusted certainty
of death—that certainty which is life, and which, through the
sudden strike of the arrow-writing, is always already deciphered
for everyone.

STANDING, in the shadow
of the stigma in the air.

Standing-for-nobody-and-nothing.
Unrecognized,
for you
alone.

With all that has room therein,
even without
language.

STEHEN, im Schatten
des Wundenmals in der Luft.

Für-niemand-und-nichts-Stehn.
Unerkannt,
für dich
allein.

Mit allem, was darin Raum hat,
auch ohne
Sprache.

This stigma in the air is something invisible and unrecognized. It cannot be touched, unlike Jesus' wounds, which convinced even the sceptical Thomas. This stigma is more "in the air"—and yet it casts a shadow, though evidently only over me, such that no one else perceives that I am standing in it. This can be stated plainly: whoever stands, stands only for himself. Standing only for oneself *[für sich allein stehen]* means standing firm *[Standhalten]*. But this suggests as well that one who stands firm does not thereby actually insist on himself *[auf sich bestehen]*. He does not stand for something or for someone; he stands, so to speak, only for himself, and for that reason, goes "unrecognized." But that is not inconsiderable. Standing and standing firm means bearing witness to something. When it says here that one is standing "even without language," it means being so alone that one no longer even communicates. But it also says, conversely, that when this I stands in the shadow of the invisible stigma and addresses itself as You, communicating absolutely "with all that has room therein," it communicates like language. Indeed, as the last verse consists of the single word "language," not only is "language" expressly emphasized, it is also "set down" *[gesetzt]*. For that reason, "even without language" means something further. Even before there is language, when one stands mutely and adheres to what even a Thomas could not doubt, there is already language. That within which the witness of standing will and should completely proclaim itself should be. It should be language. And this language, like the unrecognized standing which stands for nobody and for nothing, will be a genuine witness precisely because it wants nothing: "for itself alone." It would be useless to be more concrete about what is witnessed here. It could be many things. But the "standing" is always one and the same— for everyone.

YOUR DREAM BUTTED by waking.
With the word-groove
notched like a screw
twelve times
in its horn

The last blow that he strikes.

The ferry up-
ward poling in the
vertical, narrow
day- chasm:

it transports
something wound-read.

DEIN VOM WACHEN stößiger Traum.
Mit der zwölfmal schrauben-
förmig in sein
Horn gekerbten
Wortspur.

Der letzte Stoß, den er führt.

Die in der senk-
rechten, schmalen
Tagschlucht nach oben
stakende Fähre:

sie setzt
Wundgelesenes über.

The poem is tightly constructed. Two "stanzas," the first and the third, are each followed by a short stanza, which functions in both cases as a kind of conclusion. The poem thus can be broken up into two halves, each invoking a completely different sphere of imagery. But they share something in common: sleep and dream, or rather, waking up. Rhythmically, the two events connected here are obviously quite different. On the one hand, the insistence of the dream, butting like a goat; on the other hand, the ferry poling painstakingly upward. Nevertheless, even if viewed differently, both aim for the same thing.

This is a provisional point of departure for the question of how to understand the poem as a whole. One must proceed from individual details. The dream has turned ornery like a billy goat. As a result, something has made its way from the dark into day. Unlike other dreams familiar to us from the dream lives of sleepers, this dream has not become ornery in the moments before waking up; quite the contrary, it turns ornery because of waking. The process of waking has thus taken too long, allowing the dream finally to turn so ornery, that ultimately something is "transported," "trans-lated" upward.* In any case it is clear that the poem does not refer, say, to an actual dream during sleep. This is made perfectly clear and unambiguous by the intriguing phrase in the last verse: "wound-read." This indicates that the dream is roused in the world of words and of reading. It therefore follows that this ornery goat, like some ram species, has a horn with a notched whorl that winds its way to a point, and that this notched groove is called a "word groove." It is thus clear that the poem describes the long-delayed, long-developing birth of the word. The horn winds around with twelve whorls to a point with which the goat strikes its last blow. The number twelve hints at a rounded unit of time, perhaps twelve months, a full year—at any rate, a long time. In other words: Waking has held down the dream already for quite some time, and the dream, stirred up, strikes its blows over and over again. Thus, to use an expression from the poem "From the Undreamed," it is like a long "waking onto" [Heranwachen]. The poem apparently wants to say that a poem is not a sudden inspiration, but that it demands long preparatory work. But the actual work on a poem, conveyed in the second image as a slow and arduously moving ferry, is not the real message of this poem. Its real message is this: what surfaces is "wound-read." "Wound-read," or wound-driven, refers to a wound produced by a reading expedition that has lasted too long. Or is there a deeper ambiguity in "wound-read"? Perhaps it refers not only to the pain of reading, excessive or futile reading, but also to the pain and the wound of what is "gathered," that is, what is painfully experienced in general, which can also mean "gleaned": gathered together, as in a gleaning of suffering?**

---

*Gadamer is drawing attention to the fact that, depending on whether the prefix is separable or inseparable, the same verb, "*übersetzen,*" can mean both "to transport" or to "translate."

**Gadamer plays on the meanings of the German verb "lesen"—"to read," and "to glean," or "to gather."

Either way, what has been transported into words, translated into words, is the poem, the text wrought out of the unconscious depths with help from a kind of dream-work.

Should we comment on other details? The intensity of the image spheres is vividly self-evident: the goat's blows, the last of which breaks through to the waking world and awakens the dream. What a reversal of dreaming and waking! And then this deep "day-chasm": like the daylight dawning in a narrow, vertical chasm, what has been collected in the dark, the "wound-read," works its way up a ladder of light, into the light—but not all at once, just as the goat could not wake up the dream with one blow. But in the end he does awaken the dream; what is transported finally emerges from the dark into the light—this is the poem.

ALLIED WITH THE PERSECUTED in a late, un-
concealed,
radiant
bond.

The morning-plumb, over-gilded,
sticks to your co-
vowing, co-
prospecting, co-
writing
heels.

MIT DEN VERFOLGTEN in spätem, un-
verschwiegenem,
strahlendem
Bund.

Das Morgen-Lot, übergoldet,
heftet sich dir an die mit-
schwörende, mit-
schürfende, mit-
schreibende
Ferse.

The first stanza speaks of the persecuted. Given the poet and the time, this can scarcely be understood without reference to Hitler's persecution of the Jews. Moreover, it seems clearer than ever that what became a poem through "co-writing" is the poet's confession. And yet it did become a poem. Even if later generations should ever forget these persecutions that took place sometime, somewhere, the poem will preserve its exact place of knowledge and complicity. For the exact place of the poem cannot be forgotten. It belongs to the human condition as such that there are victims with whom one no longer completely belongs (in "late" alliance), and yet to whom one declares such complete loyalty ("un-concealed") that the alliance with them can be called "radiant," meaning unreserved and committed, as well as luminous and reflective of genuine solidarity—like light.

The second stanza also speaks of light, if in a strangely distorted way. Undoubtedly one should think of the dawn [*Morgenrot*]—when the poem refers to the "morning-plumb" [*Morgen-Lot*]. But why is the morning-plumb "over-gilded" (and not golden)? The morning-plumb seems to mean that the dawn, with which both the day and the future arise, can only begin the true future when it is experienced as a plumb-line, that is, as a straight, unerring standard of justice. This plumb-line weighs heavily. It is called over-gilded, meaning that under the golden shimmer of day and future promised by the morning there is heaviness, the weight of experience [*Erfahrung*] and the alliance with the persecuted. And this weight is itself something that pursues one, makes one into a victim.

This is expressed unequivocally by the phrase in the second stanza "stick to one's heels." The morning-plumb is like a persecutor. What does that mean? Is it a reproach against oneself for having even experienced the morning, for having a future instead of dying in solidarity? Yet even if one knows it to be all too near, the poem says nothing about dying. Indeed, it would be scarcely appropriate to see in every case an injustice in surviving. But it could be a constant admonition that persecutes by reminding one not to forget the persecuted and to take responsibility for them and for the future of humankind.

The poem's progression makes this last meaning predominant. For the heels onto which the morning-lead sticks, these heels which have turned to flight because they are constantly pursued by the morning-lead, are said to be "co-vowing, co-prospecting, co-writing." This is a precise climax within a unified direction of significance: bear witness, uncover, corroborate. But the question is: with whom should "you" co-vow (rather than flee)? In this context, clearly with the persecuted and their suffering, to whom the You openly declares loyalty. Fate is like an oath, a message which cannot be ignored, and so "co-vow" does not primarily mean bearing witness to what happened— after all, what sticks to the heel is the morning-plumb, the standard for the future. It thus means an oath for the future: never again.

The second adjective in the verse is no less significant. Prospecting occurs when something is not found in the open and must be instead uncovered, or processed from unrefined material into a pure extraction. Perhaps this is the yield that remains after suffering injustice and pain. If the third segment of this climax is then "co-writing," every reader will immediately think of the poet, who has declared himself to be in alliance with the persecuted, and who avows himself to be persecuted, neither able nor permitted to free himself from his alliance with them. The heels of the writer would like to hurry away into a realm of friendlier imagination, a world of poetry perhaps, and yet the writer is held fast, as if by a lead weight, to his task of bearing written witness to his alliance with the persecuted. That could very well be the meaning, in which case the climax would be comprehensible.

But a few questions remain open. First: can the intensification that must be present in this climax really be understood in this way? If so, in contrast to the prospecting and vowing, "co-writing" would have to mean the most direct attesting to and securing of the message. But such a view is contradicted by the triple enjambment: the isolated "co" must have the same meaning in all three cases. Yet unlike "co-writing," co-vowing and co-prospecting cannot mean directly holding fast to the exact wording of a text. The climax must thus be articulated differently. Just as he vows and prospects with the others, the speaker also wishes to write with them. If one hesitates to recognize the obvious intensification that inheres in the confession of writing and the confession of poetry as the complete sense of the poem as a whole, then the following consideration may help: with whom should "you" actually vow and write? With the persecuted? As we have seen, this can certainly be understood to mean that their suffering was itself like an oath or like a message fixed for everyone and for all time. But if so, I would ask whether that must all be added? Is it not found directly in the text, namely, in the morning-plumb? For the morning-plumb actually proclaims the day, and if it does so for everyone, and if this day should be the day of justice *[Tag des Rechtes]*, a day of measuring-up *[Lot-Rechten]*, which proclaims to everyone the injustice of the past, then is it not exactly right to think that what sticks to your heels is this dawn/morning-plumb, and that with it, with the awareness and obligation it has irrevocably placed upon everyone, you co-vow, co-prospect, and co-write? If so, then the poet's writing is, in fact, supreme, and the intensification of the speech aims toward it because it does not only refer to the poet's activity, it is a co-operation *[Mit-Tun]* in which we must all participate if there is to be a future. Who am I and who are You?

❖ ❖ ❖

THREAD-SUNS
above the gray-black wasteland.
A tree-
high thought
strikes the light-sound: there are
still songs to sing beyond
humankind,

FADENSONNEN
über der grauschwarzen Ödnis.
Ein baum-
hoher Gedanke
greift sich den Lichtton: es sind
noch Lieder zu singen jenseits
der Menschen.

Vast spaces are opened up by the great gesture of this short poem. We are reminded of a meteorological phenomenon that we all have observed at some point: the way that threads of light open up light-spaces and light-distances above the gray-black wasteland of a horizon covered over with thick clouds. It has been suggested that "thread-suns" are suns that have become as thin as threads, suns no longer round, as in better days, but this seems to me rather vague and abstract. Certainly it is a spiritual horizon (and not a weather condition) in which these thread-suns are found to draw open the gray-black wasteland. But should that inhibit one from thinking about the threads which draw the sun through the edges of heavy cloud cover? After all, we speak of the sun drawing water.* And does not this "heavenly drama" *["der Himmel Trauerspiel"]* possess something exalting for everybody; is this experience of the sublime not accessible to everybody? It is striking that "thread-suns" is a plural form—a plural that suggests the anonymous expanse of infinite worlds. Profiled against this backdrop is the singularity and uniqueness of the thought that rises up. For this is what the poem plainly declares: the monumental spaces opened up in this heavenly drama can allow one to forget the disconsolate human horizon, truly a horizon in which nothing sublime is visible any more. It is thus a tree-high thought that arises here. This thought does not grope around uselessly in the wasteland of the human world; it has grown equal to the scale of the heavenly drama and reaches the sky, like a tree. It strikes the light-sound. Reached in this way, the light-sound is, however, a song-sound. The tree-high thought which "strikes" this light-sound while lavished by the surrounding drama of the thread-suns has grown to a scale beyond all human standards and necessities, like a tree that has grown into a giant.

This sets up the poem's real message: "There are still songs to sing beyond humankind."

---

*According to Grimm, the German expression *"die Sonne zieht Wasser"* can be used to describe the bright strips seen in the sky when the sun appears through a thick cloud. There is no equivalent English expression.

IN THE SNAKE-CARRIAGE, on
past the white cypress,
through the flood
they drove you.

But in you, from
birth,
the other spring foamed,
along the black
stream memory
dayward you climbed.

IM SCHLANGENWAGEN, an
der weißen Zypresse vorbei,
durch die Flut
fuhren sie dich.

Doch in dir, von
Geburt,
schäumte die andre Quelle,
am schwarzen
Strahl Gedächtnis
klommst du zutag.

The poem is broken up into two sentences. They form two
stanzas. Once again, as is so often the case in these short poems,
what unifies both stanzas is an almost epigrammatic antithesis
introduced with a "but."

The first stanza describes intoxication with life. For what is
evoked here by the snake-carriage is Dionysus, god of drunken-
ness. It is the journey of life, which begins with devotion to
everything the senses have to offer. The white cypress is isolated
by the line break. If at first the journey of life passes by the white
cypress, perhaps this means that the intoxication with life also
colors over death. The black death-symbol of the cypress towers
like a luminous white pillar carelessly overshot by someone

drenched with life. The journey leads through the flood, the ceaseless surging wave of sensuous experience. It remains unclear who the leader of this journey through the flood is. But the plural "they" makes one thing certain: the journey is not conducted by "I." The nominative "I" does not appear in the entire poem, although it is quite clear that the poem speaks of no one else but me, every I. At first, however, each of us is not I, but something simply carried along, and the poem describes this experience of how "I" becomes I. This is why the emphasis in the poem is on the one-word verse "birth," the starting point of the becoming-I.

A turn inward is taken with the use of the adversative "but." What is depicted is how sensuous being carried along by the flood of life develops into the human I. This is like an anti-movement to offset the inundation of the senses, and the poem thus speaks of the "other spring." It "foams" on from birth. This means that, even where we don't know it, it foams out of the unfathomable spring, and indeed, does so incessantly. Moreover, it is experienced truly as a spring, not as a dazzling flood that completely envelops one, unlike the glistening and shimmering waves of sensuous experience. This "other spring" is more like something that comes out of the dark, and is called a "black stream." It is astonishing how the sensuous power of these verses allows the poet to use a word as conceptually burdened as "memory" [Gedächtnis] without becoming the least bit didactic. Memory is the ascending black stream, not the broad flood of accumulated intellectual property. And, in fact, the "I" is formed not in accumulated knowledge [Wissen], but in this stream emanating from the dark depths of the unconscious. Addressing itself, "I" climbs along it toward day; in other words, memory, one's inner knowledge of oneself, does not simply ascend like the broad flood of the senses flowing out of the first life spring. Instead, "I" works arduously upward, step by step, into the brightness of the "I" that has become aware of itself. In the end, it will become a You. This is the beginning of self-consciousness. But it cannot happen without the black stream of memory continuing to foam just as far as the raging flood of the senses.

One must note how the white of the second verse and the black of the third verse from the end answer each other. The cypress, too, will win back its natural color, its true symbolic meaning, in the black stream of memory. Knowing oneself means knowing what death is.

❖ ❖ ❖

ARMORED-RIDGES, fold-axes,
Breakthrust-
points:
your terrain.

At both poles
of the cleft-rose, legible:
your banished word.
North-true. South-bright.

HARNISCHSTRIEMEN, Faltenachsen,
Durchstich-
punkte:
dein Gelände.

An beiden Polen
der Kluftrose, lesbar:
dein geächtetes Wort.
Nordwahr. Südhell.

Two statements are juxtaposed that correspond to each other: terrain and word. "Your terrain" is the terrain of "your" word. The two stanzas thus go together. Contrary to the mistaken first impression that made its way into the first edition of this little book, the image sphere does not change. This is not about a fencer ready to fight and then a helmsman who holds his course unerringly steady. The unusual expressions "armored-ridges," "fold-axes" and "Breakthrust-points" in the first stanza, as well as the expression "cleft-rose" in the second stanza, led me astray. They belong together and stem from the same semantic field. All of them are geological terms. One thus immediately deduces, as I might have, that the first three expressions describe formations of the earth's crust. Yet, as I saw correctly, they also refer to the armor of language. The terrain is the terrain of the word. As I see more clearly now, these are all descriptions of terrain, its faults and encrustations and those points where a deeper layer has broken through the surface.

There is nothing else in these strange expressions. I went too far when I wrote the following: "The first world, the world of the sword-brandishing word, is not seen as an opposition between two fighters, but rather as one, as the word which probes and then attempts to pierce through armor. The word is a 'sword' which seeks out where the armor can be pierced. Whose armor? The armor worn by all who speak? This is what the poem seems to be about: piercing through the armor of language toward truth."

That something wasn't quite right was indicated by the fact that I could understand armored-ridges only as the ridges formed on the body by the armor, while the fold-axes and breakthrust-points had to mean the armor itself. Since then I've learned that this martial-sounding description of terrain uses standard geological terms. The poet was obviously inspired by their poetic qualities. The expressions hint at the poet's—any poet's—relationship to language. It is a question of the armor of language and the potential for reification inherent in language. My difficulties with the connection between armored-ridges and fold-axes now prove to be unfounded: this is how the geologist describes the earth's crust. It was thus false to think that "breakthrust-points" referred to the searching glance of the swordsman who tries to pierce through his enemy's armor. Like the others, this expression was also not a baroque invention of the poet's, but a geological term-of-art. Yet this language is also concerned with describing the stratification and classification of the earth's crust on the basis of the visible formations that orientate the geologist in her task of fathoming the secret of the earth's interior.

Orientation is the key word, and none other: orientation with respect to existing land formations that show the history of how the earth's surface was formed—orientation thus in the terrain of language, which is reified in its formations, in grammar, usage, sentence construction and the formation of opinion. There are firm rules and conventions for everything, and yet there are also points where it is possible to fathom deeper layers. In these expressions, especially "breakthrust," the image of the swordsman who tries to pierce through armor will simply not occur to anyone familiar with geological terminology.* But I was not wrong to the extent that the poem describes the poet's experience with language whenever he tries to break through rigid conventions of usage and "empty chatter" *["Gerede"]*. The "geological" correction was more useful to me in the second stanza. Here the predominant image sphere remains orientation with respect to terrain. "Cleft-rose" is a geological term for an orientation instrument which, like the compass, points to a scale. Every student of geology knows it, so that in this case our *poeta doctus* had no need of a lexicon or reference work. Once again it is a question of the orientation needed by the poet's word. To follow the direction suggested by the poem, undoubtedly the North and South poles mentioned in the first and last lines of the stanza, bring into play the navigator's compass, and with it, finding and holding the correct course—even if one isn't on the open seas. In fact, I am still not sure how the geologist actually uses this land compass called a "cleft-rose," but I think the poem exempts us from having to make any other special inquiries of the geologist. Indeed, the poem invites us to make a shift, and this shift leads explicitly into the sphere of language. This is unambiguous here. For it says: "your banished word." The word is "banished." This is not simply a strong expression for disdain or scorn. It also means: hated and persecuted. To be banished means to have no legal home, to be banned and thus outlawed. Now the text apparently says that this word has been banned unjustly: this word is precisely the one which keeps a steady course and which cannot be diverted by anything from the right course, the course of justice. Unalterably clear and incorruptibly, it moves along the course indicated by the "cleft-rose."

The stanza says that this "cleft-rose" is supposed to be legible at both poles, North and South. The word must be familiar, as it were, with the entire scale of possible deviations that threaten it. This outlawed word, itself unprotected, should be legible at both poles. As a result, the word "banished" obtains here a precise meaning: the word is left on its own—shunned

---

*In the German, Gadamer's point is clearer: "Durchstich," which refers to a chasm or tunnel, can be literally rendered as "through-thrust."

by all, deemed undesirable by all sides—because of the straightness
of the truth it proclaims. This means that the word is both true:
North-true, and bright: South-bright. But this word is also "your"
word. Who is addressed here? In Celan's poems (or perhaps any
poem?), there is certainly no firm principle for answering the
question "who am I, and who are you." I do not believe one
should think of a You in these poems only when they speak of
a You, or that one should think of the poet only when he says
"I." Both seem wrong to me. Might not an I say You to itself?
And who is I? I is never simply the poet. It is always also the
reader. In his Meridian speech, Celan correctly emphasized the
character of a poem as I-forgetting *[Ichvergessenheit]*. Then whose
word is it? The poet's? the poem's? Is it a word that the poem
only repeats and proclaims? Or is it perhaps a word that we all
know? What "yours" and, by implication, "you," mean is certainly
not set from the very beginning. Orientation in the terrain of
language does not have to be provided, as I had originally
assumed, by a kind of self-address on the part of the poet or
poem. It might also be, say, the word of God bursting through
the right breakthrust-point in the earth's armor—as revelation.
"Your banished word" could even refer to the Ten Command-
ments of the Old Testament, which as a North-South axis are
supposed to provide secure orientation. Or maybe it refers to
any true word whatsoever. Accordingly, one might have ultimately no reason at all for distinguishing between the word of
the true God, the word of the true poet, and the true word itself.

Here Celan has provided us with something of a confirma-
tion in his Meridian speech, where among the aspirations of
poetry, he includes: "speaking on behalf of the other—who knows,
perhaps on behalf of the 'wholly Other.' " Celan explicitly repeats
the allusion to the "wholly Other," Rudolf Otto's term for the
Holy in the history of religion. The poem can thus also be both
the true word and the banished word. In the crust of empty
chatter it recognizes "breakthrust-points"—only then does it succeed as a poem, and the poet might well call his word banished—even after being honored with the Büchner prize.* We do
not need to ask ourselves: Who am I and who are You? The
poem will say 'yes' to every answer. Now the two stanzas con-

*Celan gave his Meridian speech on the occasion of receiving the Büchner
prize in 1960.

stitute a perfect unity. It is a question of orientation in the terrain of language. Just as the formations that emerge on the surface permit the geologist to guess at rather than reach the earth's depths, so the word of the poem, left on its own, seeks to fathom hidden depths by following its true compass.

❖ ❖ ❖

WORD-DEPOSIT, volcanic,
sea-overroared.

Above,
the surging mob
of anti-creatures: it
hoisted a flag—image and after-image
cruise vainly timewards.

Until you hurl away the
word-moon, from which
the miracle ebb originates
and the heart-
shaped crater
nakedly bears witness to the beginnings,
to the king-
births.

WORTAUFSCHÜTTUNG, vulkanisch,
meerüberrauscht.

Oben
der flutende Mob
der Gegengeschöpfe: er
flaggte—Abbild und Nachbild
kreuzen eitel zeithin.

Bis du den Wortmond hinaus-
schleuderst, von dem her
das Wunder Ebbe geschieht
und der herz-
förmige Krater
nackt für die Anfänge zeugt,
die Königs-
geburten.

The conclusion to the poem cycle is formed by two poems: "Word-deposit" and "Etched away." In between are four verses set in parentheses which are made somewhat peculiar by certain distinguishing stylistic features, namely, their conventional meter and rhyme scheme.

Like many other poems in this cycle, this poem is also controlled by a simple antithesis. It speaks of the event of the word as if it were speaking about a volcanic explosion which sets it apart from the everyday activity of speaking.

The complete landscape is described immediately in the preamble: the word-deposit is rock of volcanic origin that comes out of the depths and lies there, cooled down, like a sea-mountain, a mountain overroared by the sea. That is how language exists: as the petrified configuration of earlier life-eruptions and as creation, which it was, covered over by the monotonously surging sea that consumes and makes everything the same. For the real rock of language no longer towers out of the foaming waters. What is visible as language is now called "anti-creatures," a surging mob, meaning without name, origin, or home. The mob "hoists a flag"; it adorns itself with something in which it takes pride but which does not, in truth, belong to it, something arbitrarily selected and displayed, like the pennant of a Sunday sailor. The "anti-creatures" cruise "timeward" on the surface of language. This means they are without direction or destination, and yet so propelled by "time" that they have no duration. They are the image and after-image of the genuine word, that is, they sound like imitations or like the echo of genuine creations—a futile activity that goes on and on, until. . . .

Everything aims toward this "until." Through the event of the new eruption the surface activity is uncovered in all its futility and illusoriness. The event of genuine language-making [Sprach-werdung] is described by a grand cosmic metaphor. "You"—that nameless You known and recognized only by whomever understands it as such—flings the word-moon away.

One must listen precisely. At first, one tends to associate the image of the moon's hurling away from the earth (until recently, a widely held theory about the moon's origin) directly with the "word-deposit," which is the hidden ground of language underneath the surging sea of speech. Yet with bold hyperbole this moon-word appears to be more moon than word. What is hurled away here cannot be the round, luminous, and perpetually new and plainly shining word itself, say the word of the new poet. The phrase "the word-moon"—as opposed to "a word-moon"—can only be understood to mean that the master of time- and earth-storms always finds the same way of laying bare the beginnings of a genuine new event of language. For indeed the poem speaks of the new gravitational pull now emanating from this moon and drying up the hidden mountain of language so as to make the true origin visible. The vast confusion of linguistic convention runs off, like brackish water. The "miracle-ebb" occurs, namely the miracle that in place of what appeared to have been an intraversable element of fluctuation there now emerges solid ground capable of providing support. Now, it says that what is dried up here lays bare the heart's crater, which bears witness to the beginnings. This means that in what has become newly visible, one finally recognizes again the force of containment and eruption out of which the poet's word has always secured its resiliency and endurance. When the poem goes on to say that what is attested to here are the "king-births," that is, the founders of dynasties, it means that whenever we speak we submit to a whole dynasty of language, a dynasty that rules us in the great creations of poetry moored in this language.

Or am I taking the poet here too literally (or not literally enough)? Yet that word-moon, apparently hurled by "You" from time to time out of the depths submerged by empty chatter, that word-moon which puts an end to the futile false production of speeches and poems, is, finally, itself both a word and round, genuine, light-reflecting rock. The gravitational pull exerted by it in controlling the tides is that of the word alone. For only the word itself can and does lay bare genuine word-rock. It thereby makes itself visible, as well as all the "beginnings" that govern our speaking as creations of poetry and disappear with the futile cruising of haphazardly propelling talk. Understood in this way, the word-moon is a symbol of the full moon-word in which all new eruptions from the volcanic ground are comprehended. The moon is thus the word itself. And it is indeed the case that we experience not only the new creation of language achieved by the poet, but that under its influence we discover anew all the royal forms of our language. These are the "king-births": something which happened a long time ago to establish authority, and whose sovereignty is again established by the new poem. Every true poem stirs the hidden depths of the ground of language and its creative formations. It recognizes authority, and establishes new authority under its own dynasty.

In any case, the metaphor wonderfully describes the true poetic word as a cosmic event—not only as something that destroys nothing of what is true and uncovers the truth, but even more so, as a word that no one, not even the poet, can claim as his own. The poet hoists no flags.

(I KNOW YOU, you are she-who-is-deeply-bowed,
I, the one-pierced-through, submit to you.
Where flames a word which for us both can vow?
You—wholly, wholly real. I—wholly illusion.)

(ICH KENNE DICH, du bist die tief Gebeugte,
ich, der Durchbohrte, bin dir untertan.
Wo flammt ein Wort, das für uns beide zeugte?
Du—ganz, ganz wirklich. Ich—ganz Wahn.)

The I that speaks here and admits in the end to being
"wholly illusion" is not transformed in these verses into that
omnipresent I of lyric poetry in which poet and reader are
fused together. The parentheses enclose it in the particularity of
the speaking-I, secluding it from the generality customarily associated with the lyrical I. It similarly encloses the addressed
You, imbuing the whole with something of the character of a
discreet dedication, or the signature of a painting such that the
motifs in these verses allude to the Pietà (deeply-bowed/pierced-
through).

But the statement of these four verses retains its firm connection to the poem cycle in which it occurs, though, to be sure,
with a gesture of retreat. The poet, who here says "I" for himself
and not for all of us, is frightened both by the demand that his
word be reality and that he proclaim the reality of one so wholly
different from himself. "Where flames a word which for us both
can vow?" sounds like a conscious resignation on the poet's part
to the fact that even the truest word cannot attain what is "wholly,
wholly real."

Yet the gesture of admission and resignation seemingly
interpolated here actually links together the two poems that form
the conclusion of "Breath-crystal." Both of them are about language, and in particular, the true language, which is the language
of the true poet.

ETCHED AWAY by the
ray-wind of your language
the garish chatter of the commonly-
experienced—the hundred-
tongued my—
poem, the noem.

Un-
drifted,
free
the path through the human-
shaped snow,
the penitents' snow, to
the hospitable
glacier-rooms and -tables.

Deep
in the time-crevice
by the
honeycomb-ice
waits, a breath-crystal,
your irrefutable
witness.

WEGGEBEIZT vom
Strahlenwind deiner Sprache
das bunte Gerede des An-
erlebten—das hundert-
züngige Mein-
gedicht, das Genicht.

Aus-
gewirbelt,
frei
der Weg durch den menschen-
gestaltigen Schnee,
den Büßerschnee, zu
den gastlichen
Gletscherstuben und -tischen.

Tief
in der Zeitenschrunde,
beim
Wabeneis
wartet, ein Atemkristall,
dein unumstößliches
Zeugnis.

The poem is clearly divided into three stanzas which do not have an equal number of verses. It is like the second act of the dramatic event evoked in "Word-deposit." The poem begins after the event that destroyed the false appearance of language. Only in this way does it become clear what is meant by "the ray-wind of your language": a wind that blows in from cosmic distances, etching away with the brightness and bite of its elemental power the chatter of the commonly experienced as if discoloring tarnish. This "chatter" here refers to all false-poems. The chatter is garish because the language of such false creations is capricious, motivated simply by the need for decorative effect, for ornament, and thus without its own color or tongue. These false creations of language speak with a hundred tongues because they are so capricious, and this means that, in reality, they bear witness to nothing—they offer, so to speak, false witness. This is the "my-poem,"* the poem which gives false oath and is a "noem," that is, which amounts to nothing at all despite appearing to be a configuration.

The talk of "ray-wind of your language" further develops the fundamental cosmic metaphor that animated the poem "Word-deposit." "Your" language is the language of the You which hurls the word-moon; thus it is not so much the language of a poet, or of this poet as such, but the appearance *[Erscheinung]* of language itself —true, luminous, and round language. It etches away all false witness, removes it so thoroughly that not a trace of it remains. In this way, "ray-wind" may invoke the cosmic dimensions of this eruption, but beyond anything else, it certainly invokes the purity and radiating brilliance—the true spirituality—of language; language which does not feign imitative and derivative statements, but rather unmasks them as such.

Only when the "wind of your language" rushes in with its radiating purity does the path to the poem begin, to the "breath-crystal," which is nothing but the configuration of pure, delicate

---

*"Mein-Gedicht" in German literally means "my-poem," but it alludes to the archaic word "*Meineid*," meaning "oath." Celan's enjambment separates the syllable "mein," meaning "my" or "mine." See Gadamer's discussion in the introduction to this volume, pp. 67–69, as well as the Epilogue, p. 137.

geometry that falls from the soft nothingness of breath. The path is now free. The single word "free" extends over the entire length of a verse, just as the syllable "un" took up an entire line. In fact, the path now free became visible as a path after the ray-wind "un-drifted" the snow that had covered everything up and made it the same. This path is like the path of the pilgrim leading to icy heights. The pilgrim strides through the "snow," that is, through everything unwelcoming, rejecting, demanding of restraint, cold, and monotonously uniform, all of which the re-pentant pilgrim dares to overcome. This vision undoubtedly has to be transposed into the linguistic sphere, for the snow through which one must stride is *human-shaped.* With all their chatter, it is people who cover everything over. But where does the path of this journey lead? Clearly not to a pilgrim's shrine, but to the glacier-world itself, where the bright, clear air accommodates the enduring pilgrim like an inn. This world of eternal ice is welcom-ing because only effort and perseverance led there, and as a result, the indiscriminate human snow-production no longer rules. The path of this journey is thus ultimately the path of the pu-rification of the word which, in the practice of silence and circumspection, renounces all popular trends and language con-ventions. This journey in the heights of the uninhabited winter mountains leads to a hospitable place. Where one is far enough away from the trends of human activity one is close to the ultimate goal, the goal of the true word.

What awaits one there still lies deeply hidden: deep in the time-crevice. This sounds like an unplumbable crevasse which has opened up in the glacial ice. Yet it is a time-crevice, a tear in the regular flow of time, at a location where time no longer flows because, like everything else, it also stands frozen in eter-nity. "By the honeycomb ice,"—the optical and acoustic vivid-ness of this is also compelling, ice-built and layered like the honeycomb in a beehive is a construction that cannot be altered, meaning that it is protected against the influences of "flowing time"—there, by this "ice," the poem, the breath-crystal, "waits." Obviously one should also perceive here a contrast between the encircling walls of ice and the tiny crystal of breath, this most fleeting existence *[Dasein]* of the geometric miracle that is the delicately marked snowflake fluttering alone in the air of a cold winter's day. This tiny detail is, nonetheless, witness. The poem calls it "irrefutable witness," apparently in stark contrast to the perjurious testimonies of "fashioned" *["gemachter"]* poems. "You" are what it testifies to ('Your' witness)—the intimate, unknown You which, for the I that here is the I of the poet as well as the reader, is its You, "wholly, wholly real."

Epilogue

L
ooking over the literary critical and scholarly resonance around Paul Celan's work as presented by D. Meineke, anyone who loves Celan's poetry must be somewhat disappointed. Whatever these experts and initiates say about Celan's work—often it is quite subtle, sometimes genuinely insightful—presupposes, irrespective of intention, that one understands the verses and judges on the basis of this understanding, for example, when making a claim about the poet's sudden muteness or his agonizing failure in a word which has become cryptic. In contrast, it seems to me not much has been done for understanding the word which has not yet fallen mute. For Celan readers, one of the most pressing tasks still remains largely unfulfilled. These readers do not need a critical judgment which denies the possibility of further understanding; they need to begin at a point where understanding becomes possible, and with an explanation of how to proceed. In the good old days, this was called *Realinterpretation.* For a poet as conscious of tradition as Celan, the value and appropriateness of this kind of interpretation should not be lightly dismissed. In no way is the point to establish the unambiguousness of the poet's intent. Neither is it to ascertain the unambiguousness of the "meaning" articulated in the verses themselves. Rather what matters is the meaning of the ambiguity and indeterminacy stirred up by the poem. Such meaning does not invite the reader's whim and fancy; it is the very center of the hermeneutic struggle demanded by these verses. Anyone familiar with the difficulty of this task knows that it cannot be a matter of naming all the connotations resonant in the "understanding" of poetic configurations, but rather of making visible

the unity of meaning which befits the text as a linguistic unity, such that the unmistakable connotations connected to it find their semantic support. With a poet who forces the distortion of natural speaking as much as Celan did, this is always full of risks and it requires critical control. This book is dedicated to an attempt clearly fraught with errors, yet a task which nothing can replace or relieve.

That I have chosen to look at the sequence "Breath-crystal," which has been published separately before and introduces the volume *Breath-turn*, can very simply be explained in the first place by the fact that I believe I have more or less understood these poems. Yet it is an old hermeneutic principle that the interpretation of difficult texts must begin where one first has a preliminary, half-way certain understanding. It remains beside the point whether, as it seems to me, the cycle of "Breath-crystal" also represents the apogee of Celan's art, thereby making it more than accidental that I believe I have understood these poems, since I find them less likely than some of his later poems to sink into the indecipherable.

I am aware that Paul Celan's world has sources quite remote from the traditions of the world in which I—as well as most of his readers—grew up. I lack basic expertise in Jewish mysticism, Hasidism (which Celan himself presumably knew only from Buber), and most of all, the folk customs of eastern European Jewry, which formed the self-evident background out of which Celan spoke. I also lack the poet's astonishingly detailed knowledge of nature, and instruction in one area or another would be often quite appreciated. And yet such instruction should give us pause. One is liable to wind up in a certain danger zone: it could happen that one summons up knowledge which perhaps the poet himself did not possess. Celan occasionally warned against such a zeal for knowledge. Even in cases where we have the benefit of knowledge or even information stemming from the poet himself, the legitimacy of such help is determined, finally, only by the poetry itself. If it is not fully redeemed by the poetry, such help is "false." Of course, every poet warrants a certain amount of study, and so even here the "language" of the poet cannot be detached from the context of his work. Perhaps the remaining drafts of Celan's poems will bring us further help—though even this sort of help would not be unambiguous, as Hölderlin's example has taught us. Generally, I think it is a sound principle not to view poetry as an arcane cryptogram for scholars, but rather as something intended for the members of a shared language community, a world in which the poet is just as much at home as his listeners or readers. When and where the poet succeeds in forming self-standing linguistic configurations, it should be possible for the poetic ear to elevate what matters to a degree of clarity independent from and beyond such particularized knowledge, and thereby approach the precision which constitutes the undisclosed mystery of this cryptic poetry.

Of course, the process of understanding a poem does not proceed on a single level. Initially it occurs on only one level: the level of words. Understanding the words is thus primary. Anyone ignorant of the language in question is immediately excluded, and since the words of a poem are the unity of a speech, a breath, and a voice, one must not only understand the meaning of individual words. On the contrary, the precise significance of a word is determined only by the unity of a figure of meaning formed by the speech. The unity possessed by the figure of meaning of poetic speech can still be dark, laden with tension, split, cracked, and brittle—the polyvalence of the words is determined in completing the meaning of the speech and permits one significance to resound and others simply to resonate. Such unambiguousness is necessarily characteristic of all speaking, even that of *poésie pure*. This should be self-evident, and it seems to me entirely wrong to deny that every word must first be understood in the precise concretion of its significance in the speech, and that this primary level of understanding cannot be circumvented. This is wholly true of Paul Celan, in whose work the individual word is stated quite concretely and precisely. What the speech says "at first" must be discovered and considered over and over again, although it is not this first level of the signifying and naming function of the words, and the unity of speech formed by them, on which the actual precision of being said *[Gesagtsein]* is achieved that allows the speech to be a poem. In truth, one cannot simply remain on this level, for various levels are always already intertwined. This is what makes the task of understanding so difficult.

But then what does it mean "to understand"? There are many different forms of "understanding" which, to a certain extent, can be completed independently of each other. Yet already classical hermeneutic theory emphasized the interrelation of these various kinds of interpretation, despite efforts like those of F. A. Boeckh in his teaching on interpretive method to keep the various methods of interpretation sharply separated from each other. This is especially true of the older teaching of the four levels of scriptural meaning, which simply describe the dimensions of understanding. But what is the *sensus allegoricus* in Celan? It is well known that Celan would not hear of there being any metaphors in his work, and if we understand metaphor as a part or a means of speech that can be lifted from or incorporated into what is actually said, this resistance is quite understandable. Where everything is metaphor, nothing is metaphor. Where the plain, precise wording "means" what we are speaking about here, not as a "positive" in the Hegelian sense, as a preexisting world of meaning and form, but rather where it means each in the other, in what is said, not at all, and in this "not," indeed nothing else—where the wording means in this sense, not only are various levels of saying differentiated, but they are bound as one even in their variety. Here there are no allegories. Everything is itself.

The poetic word is "itself" in the sense that nothing other, nothing prior, exists against which it can be measured. And yet there is no word which does not exist beyond itself; that is, there is no word, which beyond its polyvalent significance and what is named by the various levels of that significance, does not yet also constitute its own being said. But this means that it is an answer. Answers comprise questions as well as resolve them. Thus the utterance *[Gesagte]* is not made up only of itself, even when nothing else beyond its realization in language is otherwise apparent.

This does not change what is incomprehensibly obligatory in a poem, namely that it stand by itself, and that it not contain a single word standing for something in such a way that another word could be substituted for it. "The true language seems to me to be that in which word and thing coincide" (G[ünther] Eich). And yet the singularity of how it is said always implies something else. Like any word in a conversation, the poem also has the character of a rejoinder [Gegenwort], which makes audible what is in fact not said, but rather presupposed as an expectation of meaning, and indeed awakened by the poem—even if only to be broken as such. This is especially true of contemporary poetry like that of Celan's. It is nothing like baroque poetry, whose statements are contained inside a uniform frame of reference and occupy a common mythological, iconographic, and semantic foundation. Celan's word choices venture upon a network of linguistic connotations whose hidden syntax cannot be acquired from anywhere else but the poems themselves. This is what prescribes the path of interpretation; one is not transported by the text into a world of meaning familiar in its coherence. Fragments of meaning seem to be wedged together; the path of transposition cannot be followed from one level of simple intentionality [Gemeintsein] to a second level of actually being said. Rather, in a way which cannot be easily described, the actual utterance is always the same as what the speech intended. What occurs with understanding is not so much transposition as the constant actualization of transpositionality, in other words, the sublation of all the "positivity" ["Positivität"] of that first level, which is, in the affirmative sense, thereby "preserved" and maintained.

This is completely decisive for Celan-interpretation—and not only for it. For this is what determines the hotly contested value of information deriving from outside the poem, information acquired from the poet's own communications, or that of his friends, and used to establish the "biographical" occasion, the biographically discernible motivation, the specific, concrete situation of a poem. It is known, not least from Celan himself in the Büchner speech, that precisely in contrast to Mallarmé's conception of art and that of his followers, Celan's poetry is a kind of word-creation and word-discovery arising like a confession from a specific life circumstance. Obviously the individual details of this circumstance cannot all be discerned from the poetic text alone. Take a poem like "Flower," the drafts of which can be examined now thanks to a study by Rolf Bücher.

FLOWER

The stone.
The stone in the air, which I followed.
Your eye, as blind as the stone.

We were
hands,
we scooped the darkness empty, we found
the word that came up summer:
flower.

Flower: a blind man's word.
Your eye and my eye:
they provide
water.

Growth.
Heart-wall upon heart-wall
leafs toward it.

One more word like this, and the hammers
will swing in the open.

BLUME

Der Stein.
Der Stein in der Luft, dem ich folgte.
Dein Aug, so blind wie der Stein.

Wir waren
Hände,
wir schöpften die Finsternis leer, wir fanden
das Wort, das den Sommer heraufkam:
Blume

Blume—ein Blindenwort.
Dein Aug und mein Aug:
sie sorgen
für Wasser.

Wachstum.
Herzwand um Herzwand
blättert hinzu.

Ein Wort noch, wie dies, und die Hämmer
schwingen im Freien.

It is a vain fantasy to imagine one could have guessed this poem was about Celan's little son, who produced the word "flower" one day, like a promise. It is plain to see that in the word "flower"—and not only the flower of the word, which in Hölderlin means "language"—the poem traces a story of growing and opening. That it is father and son who grow toward each other here must simply be known. But no: it does not need to be known. It is also a property of the sequence of transpositional levels in this poem that the singularity of the particular occasion passes over into a certain universality which makes the poem absolutely accessible to everybody. Growing toward one another can occur in a wide range of different constellations: in the spirituality of a thought which awakens the dead to life; in the imminence of a lovers' embrace which brings the dead eye that had blazed briefly like a meteor to radiant bloom; in stone, star, and flower; or, as the poet seems to have "intended," in the growing devotion between father and son, when the child seems to awaken from an inanimate existence in which his eye is still like stone and emerges into the growing word-world of looking and exchanging glances. Who would want to presume that only the latter, and nothing else, can be found in this poem? Moreover: does "knowing" what the poet had in mind therefore mean one knows what the poem says? I am convinced that it is a serious mistake for one to think it is an advantage to have in mind what is "correct," a mistake which Celan himself would have been the last to support. He insisted that a poem must be left to its own existence and detached from its creator. Whoever does not understand more than what the poet could have said without his poetry understands far too little.

Of course, outside information can be often valuable. It protects against blatant error in the attempt to interpret. It makes it easier to understand everything correctly, that is, with uniform coherence, at least on a preliminary level. But Celan's poems cannot be understood as poems by remaining on one level or another. Celan is supposed to have said once that his poems contained only a variety of possible beginnings, not gaps. This would suggest that the same poem could be comprehensible with coherence and precision on a number of transpositional levels.

Thus it seems to me that the poem "Flower" is comprehensible on various levels. And if one thinks about the question I raised in relation to the poem cycle "Breath-crystal": Who am I and who are you?— does anybody really want to answer it? I must insist that the figure of this You is itself, not any particular person, a beloved, or any other, even the Wholly Other.

What has been attempted here, the interpretation of a cycle of Celan's poems without any special kind of information, certainly remains risky. But I repeat the phrase "special kind," for in itself the mass of information which all readers have for themselves is in many ways already "specialized." What one person knows from experience, another knows only from books. One person knows about, say, the German-Slavic East, Jewish ritual, or even Kabbalistic mysticism; another finds orientation only by using a lexicon, or through arduous reading. This is also true of the associative reference to what has been said before. One person hears George and Rilke, as perhaps the poet did, or even French language and poetry, again perhaps as the poet did; another does not. One person knows from his or her own language usage a technical expression used by the poet; another can only become familiar with it slowly. Such specialties are constantly in play. In that sense, even the special specialty represented by knowing private information about the poet is really not quite so special. No reader can understand without specialties, and yet every reader understands only when the specialty of the occasion is sublated by the universality of occasionality. This means that the poem does not bring to language a specific, unique occurrence known only to witnesses or those enlightened by the poet directly. It means that every reader can respond to what the language gesture conjures up, as if it were an offer. All readers must supplement what they can perceive in a poem on the basis of their own experience. This alone is what it means to understand a poem.

But when the drafts left to us in Celan's estate are so informative, as in the case of the aforementioned poem "Flower," shouldn't they be used wherever possible to protect against error? Isn't it a bit dangerous to try and "understand" on one's own? I am far from dismissing the help which these drafts can provide. Even so, the proper use of them also presupposes prior engagement, prior understanding, and sincere, probing meditation on the text itself. Moreover, every poet must be granted the freedom not to have passed through these drafts in a logical manner. The interpretive value of drafts must be proven by the finished text. These drafts may well hold historical interest, but do not lead the way for interpreting the finished poem. The image conveyed by an inquiry into the drafts of "Flower" reveals the making of the poem to be a process of ongoing compression, abbreviation and omission. This recalls Mallarmé, who once said that the chief task of genuine poetry was to omit, removing as much of the beginning and the conclusion of every thought as possible in order to allow readers the enjoyment of being able to find the means of completing the whole themselves. I don't think this accurately describes Mallarmé's poetic method, nor am I at all inclined to grant authority to a poet's self-interpretation. For plainly it is not so much a matter of omission as of compression.* Even the drafts of "Flower" reveal not only simple omissions, but also intensification and condensation. It is as if the disunity of the words and parts of speech increases the potency of the elements of the utterrance, such that they say more and radiate in more directions than they could in taut syntactical wrapping. Mallarmé's comment about "omission" is thus right in the sense that a poem is able to complete itself on the strength of its linguistic compression, and that its poetic construction and its motivic direction *[motivische Führung]* contribute more to understanding than what it seems to express in its words alone. A good poem is distinguished from a mysterious work of magic by the fact that the more one fathoms its composition and the technique that produces its effect, the more one is convinced of its precision. The more precisely one understands, the more richly

---

*The German verb *verdichten* means "to condense" or "solidify." It contains the root *dichten*, which means "to write poetry." Gadamer uses this word play to suggest that the poet, the *Dichter*, is one who compresses.

associative and meaningful the act of poetic creation becomes. Here structuralist analysis has observed something true. Yet by limiting itself to the sound-image *[Lautgestalt]*, such analysis neglected to mediate the "structure" exhibited in the tension-laden framework of sound and meaning with the text's unified conception of meaning *[einheitliche Sinnmeinung]*. These are, of course, tasks which simultaneously demand the highest degree of aural sensitivity and the utmost intellectual acuity.

Matters become far worse when the textual basis of the finished text available in print is shown to be wrong. Much to my chagrin, this occurs once in the sequence I have chosen. Looking through the privately printed version of "Breath-crystal" I suddenly discovered that the second verse of the third poem contained "heaven's coin" rather than "heaven's acid." I was assured that Celan himself had labelled the familiar form of the text a transcriptive mistake that had somehow crept into the later printings, and that he recognized and corrected it much later—incidentally, without much fuss. Naturally, the textual error makes the interpreter subject to false inferences. That was true for me, and thus I had to look for the correct inferences on this new basis—certainly an interesting circumstance which shows the degree of certainty pertaining to the precise coherences one thought one had discovered. Yet it remains a question just how much the overall understanding of the poem is modified by something like that. In general, one can say that a poem's framework of coherence *[Kohärenzgefüge]* is borne by so many supports that the replacement of individual supports will not cause the framework as a whole to collapse completely. Only praxis can determine whether that happens in specific instances. In any case, it seems to me that the risk of these uncertainties with respect to the basis of the text is relatively harmless compared to the risk borne by interpretation as such. Yet even this is no reason to refrain from attempting what is possible. The poems are there. In attempting to understand them, the reader will not be consoled by the prospect of relying on the critical edition or the results of "research." Instead, he or she will try to complete the "partial" understanding upon which for any reader the attraction of these poems depends.

There remains another hermeneutically interesting debate raised by the cycle I have interpreted. This is the word *Meingedicht* ["false poem"]. Quite serious readers have understood this to mean the poem that remains stuck in what is mine *[im Meinen]*, the poem that is "mine" in the sense of remaining private. In fact, this assumption yields a considerable coherence of meaning not far off the mark. Now I hear that Celan himself repudiated this undoubtedly incorrect interpretation of *Meingedicht*. But let us assume for the moment that he had clearly accepted this other, not altogether implausible interpretation. Would his say then be decisive? I don't think so. For one can explain why *Meingedicht* must be understood here to mean false witness, as in a "false oath" *[Meineid]*. It is because the poem thereby attains a higher degree of coherence and greater precision. Understood in that sense, *Meingedicht* offers an exact contrast to the "irrefutable witness" which concludes the poem. Naturally, I was not surprised that Celan had understood his poem correctly. But it is not always so clear, especially when, as in this case, the false understanding does not seriously disrupt the coherence of the whole, but at worst leads to a reduction of precision. One might also imagine a case in which the poet does not understand himself correctly, in other words, in which he vouches for an interpretation—it does not matter whether it comes from him or from others—that is also plausible, and yet clearly as incorrect as the false interpretation of *Meingedicht*. In such a case, the text ultimately holds authority over the poet. This is not as monstrous as it sounds. Think, for example, of the aging Goethe's famous error—actually, he was not so horribly old when he mistook his Prometheus poem for a part of his fragmentary Prometheus drama. Since I had no access to private information with respect to the Celan cycle interpreted here, such reflections remain for the moment purely theoretical. The point is to clarify the sense in which a poem is detached from its creator—so detached that its creator can, perhaps even must, fall short of it. "My word is no longer mine."

Among the papers left behind by Peter Szondi, we read his study of a poem from Celan's "Schneepart" [Snowpart] which alludes to the murder of Karl Liebknecht and Rosa Luxemburg.* Here Szondi imparts irrefutably precise biographical details in order to "decipher" the poem, while at the same time disavowing any recourse to this factual material: "Nothing indeed would be a greater betrayal of the poem and its author." Szondi then attempts to reconstruct by himself the logic of the poem. Unfortunately, this unfinished fragment is all that we have left from him.

And yet since Szondi formulated these questions so pointedly, he invites us even now to continue the conversation with him. When he cites Jakobson and correctly contrasts a kind of "nexus provided by the linguistic material" [vom Sprachmaterial bereitgestelltes Ineinander] to the sequence of the statement of the sentence [Nacheinander der Satzaussage], he cannot simultaneously deny this sequence and its semantic claim.** But how can we make good on this claim without information?

Perhaps we don't need the special information Szondi possessed and communicated to us. But how much can we understand without it? First of all, one must realize that no reader is completely without information. Neither the fictional null point of complete ignorance, nor the universal accessibility of information, can be a meaningful standard for the poem and its reader; neither can Szondi's special biographical knowledge. Then how much must one know? Let us put some concrete questions to Celan's poem.

---

*See the fragment entitled "Eden" in Peter Szondi's Schriften II (Frankfurt: Suhrkamp Verlag, 1977).

**The quote is from Szondi himself, who refers to Jakobson's distinction between metonymy and metaphor (ibid., p. 398).

YOU ARE LYING in the great Listening,
surrounded by bushes, by flakes.

You, go to the Spree, go to the Havel,
go to the meat hooks,
to the red stakes of apples
from Sweden —

Here comes the table with gifts,
it curves around an Eden—

The man became a sieve, the woman
had to swim, the pig,
for herself, for no one, for everyone—

The Landwehrkanal will not rush.
Nothing
  stops.

DU LIEGST im großen Gelausche,
umbuscht, umflockt.

Geh du zur Spree, geh zur Havel,
geh zu den Fleischerhaken,
zu den roten Äppelstaken
aus Schweden—

Es kommt der Tisch mit den Gaben,
er biegt um ein Eden—

Der Mann ward zum Sieb, die Frau
mußte schwimmen, die Sau,
für sich, für keinen, für jeden—

Der Landwehrkanal wird nicht rauschen.
Nichts
  stockt.

That the poem is about Berlin can be recognized by anyone through the references to the Spree and the Havel. Moreover, anyone who has been there knows that Berlin has a Landwehrkanal, and if not, one can easily find out. But that is all. Knowing that the catchword "Landwehrkanal" designates that horrible political assassination of January 1917 is much less common. How does the reader proceed? The provocative word "bitch," and its association with the Landwehrkanal, makes what happened quite clear: murder. Thus it is also clear what it means for the man to have become a sieve. A man and a woman were shot there, and the woman was thrown into the canal. That the "pig" *[Sau]* refers to a Jewish woman surely does not have the character of a quotation, despite what eager young philologists may think today (this is also the case with "sieve," although it is true Celan found both in an account of the trial). Rather, as older readers will recognize, the word is a markedly anti-Semitic insult. Celan understood it that way, not as a literary reference. So far, so good. Yet obviously if this is all one knows, one has understood far too little. Even if the vulgarity and hate of the murderers are discernible in the words, one must know to whom these feelings were directed, or at least make the attempt to find out. This is plainly necessary. For it is perfectly clear, and sharply accentuated by the conclusion "the Landwehrkanal will not rush," that this must be about a unique and horrible event. But what else?

What can still be learned from the poem itself? "Surrounded by bushes" and "surrounded by flakes" may well be associated with winter in Berlin, but certainly not with the view through his bedroom window which Celan had during his visit. Bush and flake are better understood in terms of protection (surrounded by bush, by flakes), and an inwardly listening stillness *[nach innen lauschende Stille]* (thus: "in the great listening" *[im großen Gelausche]*).

And in "here comes the table with gifts" will one hear a reference to the atmosphere of the days just before Christmas? Probably not. It will be understood more generally to contrast and contradict the horror conjured up by what follows. Here the bold phrase "it curves around an Eden" is especially helpful. Who? The table? The Advent joy? Once again, it cannot be associated with either the old or the new Hotel Eden until that concrete reference is acquired through additional information. All the same, what continues after "it curves around an Eden" creates a bitter contrast to an opulent table of gifts. No matter what kind of Eden it is—perhaps it is even the opulent festival itself—it is the goal neither of this journey, nor of the gifts to come. "Curving around an Eden" is a path which leads away from happiness, not towards it. This is what the poem tells about, not the poet's automobile trip past the new Hotel Eden.

Thus the intensification of contrastive tension is decisive for the poem. Can one also hear it in the previous verses (the way a reader informed by Szondi can)? Certainly—there is for example a contrast between the meat hooks and the "red stakes of apples from Sweden." The red that comes from the apples and (perhaps one can guess this) their being offered up on stakes, stands in bloody contrast to the "meat hooks." But this still does not bring one to the depiction of the chamber of horrors at Plötzensee on the Havel. Can this be surmised in any way? According to Szondi's report, the poet himself went "to the Havel" and to the meat hooks at Plötzensee. But let us agree: this should not be introduced as a biographical fact. This is confirmed by the imperative form of "go." People are required to see it all for themselves. But what exactly should be seen? Do we know? Isn't the poem comprehensible without knowing anything of Plötzensee, Liebknecht, and Rosa Luxemburg?

Really?

We agreed that the crude murder scene depicted at the end points the reader to a unique event, and that not being able to surmise what the poem refers to on the basis of this knowledge and information means that one does not know enough—in the poem's terms. For the poem intends us to know this event. So much so, that the last two verses, the last two words of the poem "nothing" and "stops," again conglomerate the horrible tension controlling the poem and cause it to explode all boundaries. Given what has come before, "nothing stops" must be heard first like this: "Everything goes on its own course, like the gentle flowing of the Landwehrkanal. No one stops to consider this monstrousness." But then all of a sudden the reader registers the line break and the self-sufficient force which "stops" acquires through it—and is stopped. Does this mean in the end that, in view of this monstrousness, the nothingness of going on leads to stagnation—or that it should lead to stagnation? Doesn't the end mean: It should not be the case that everything just goes on?

If so, then the poet has really given something of himself—and not as someone who happened to be listening out his window in Berlin on a winter's night, surrounded by the day's impressions: Plötzensee and the festive Christmas market of contemporary Berlin; reading the account of the Liebknecht and Luxemburg murders; one Hotel Eden recalling another, and the horror witnessed there. The sequence of the imperatives "You, go to the Spree, go to the Havel/ Go to the meat hooks" is not simply a demand for all people to see and know it all for themselves. Even more, it is a demand for one to become aware how all these contradictions can be present so close together: the Spree and the horrible ghosts of the Havel; the awful meat hooks and the colorful excitement of Christmas; the luxury hotel on the site of a tragedy—this is all there simultaneously. This is all there—horror and joy, Eden and Eden. Nothing stops—nothing at all? Here, it seems to me, lies the hidden answer to Szondi's daring question.

One need not know anything private and ephemeral. Even if one does, one must forget it and concentrate only on what the poem knows. The poem, for its part, wants us to know, learn, and experience everything that it knows—and never to forget it.

Concerning the question about the intrinsic value of information, the following should be emphasized: the tension between special information and information obtained from the poem itself is not only relative, as shown above; it is also variable, in the sense that it weakens during the course of a work's reception. Many things become so completely familiar that in the end everyone knows them. For example, think of what occasioned Goethe's Sesenheim Friederike poems. But they also change. Perhaps some of Celan's poems will open up for us only when new information becomes available, for example, from extant drafts, the knowledge of friends, or the fruits of directed research. We are still just beginning a path upon which poets have been known occasionally to venture ahead of their readers by providing an explanation. One thinks of Rilke's "Killing is a

<u>figure of our wandering sorrow</u>" (*Sonnets to Orpheus*, Book 2, Pt. 17). A poet gradually enters into the common consciousness of the reader the more his unique sound sings in our ears and his world becomes our world. This is certainly possible, and in the case of Celan, perhaps we should even expect it. But this does not allow us to take the second step before the first—and the first step remains wanting to understand what the poem tells us.

There is one other motivation, and that is precisely what we have just been considering: what everyone should know is exhorted in the poem presented by Szondi in such a way that, in the end, every reader does know. With his poem, the poet creates memory.

This brings us to a decisive point for any art of interpretation, one that concerns the hermeneutic value of scholarship. The matter demands utmost clarity. A number of things must be distinguished.

There is no contradiction in accepting in one case all the various possible interpretations which resonate in the linguistic gesture of the poem, and in other cases privileging one of these as "correct" because it is more precise. These are two different things: the process of approximation toward "correctness," which is the goal of every interpretation, and the convergence and equivalence of the levels of understanding, all of which are "correct." The precision of an autobiographical understanding is as such no greater than that of an abstract and more stringently detached understanding. This is because the deeper certainty of particularity which the reader gains from private biographical or exegetical information does not as such increase the precision of the poem. Precision is a keen measure of what is measurable. Only the latter provides a standard of measure, and there is no question that the level of the poem concerning which the author gives private information is not the level in which the poem itself is established as a standard. Thus a reader armed with these sorts of facts may indeed recognize them in the poem in a precise manner. But this does not constitute understanding the poem, and may not even lead to such understanding. The real standard of measure would be that precision in the understanding of a poem attained by the ideal reader only on the basis of the poem itself and the knowledge he or she possesses. Only when an autobiographically informed mode of understanding fully includes this precision can the various levels of understanding be present together—something Szondi correctly understood. This is the only standard of measure which protects against a betrayal of the private.

I also believe it is entirely wrong to think that the precision required by such understanding must or ought to be rejected because it is unscholarly and apt to lapse into groundless impressions. It is true that impressions are not interpretations, and that they constitute the uncertainty of every interpretation. One must admit that the syntax of connotations at play here is often registered merely through vague associations, and that a precise realization does not often result. Yet so-called scholarly aids such as the comparison or juxtaposition of parallels are not much better. Every method of interpretation can fail. The common source of all such failures is that one obstructs one's way to the poem by attempting to understand it on the basis of something external, something brought in from the outside, or even one's own subjective impressions. This sort of understanding is mired in the subjective. Its claim to constitute understanding is hybrid, whether it is based on subjective impressions or private information. Even the latter remains dangerous enough if it is granted full value. With respect to Celan's work, a confession of incomprehension is, in most cases, a commandment of scholarly integrity.

Thus one ought not be frightened by the prospect of failure, but instead try to say how one understands—with the risk that one sometimes misunderstands, or gets mired in the vagueness of untrustworthy impressions. Only in this way do others have a chance to profit from one's effort. Such profit does not so much inhere in the fact that the onesidedness of one's own attempt provokes a counter-onesidedness, but in the fact that the text's space of resonance as a whole is thereby extended and enriched.

The logic of connotations has its own stringency. It certainly does not have the unambiguousness of proofs or deductive systems, but neither does it have the arbitrariness of private associations. One feels it when understanding succeeds. Everything in the text tightens up, the degree of coherence is unmistakably increased, as well as the overall cohesion of the interpretation. So long as coherence does not extend fully to the whole of a given text, everything can still go wrong. But if the unity of the speech becomes comprehensible as a whole, a certain criterion of correctness is achieved. Even in a poetic configuration, coherence is undoubtedly a supreme condition. Obviously, such coherence does not depend on preconceived ideas of symmetry or regularity, and the demand for it is certainly not without ambiguity. As we saw above, the text can always still unfold into various levels of understanding. But each of these levels has its own complete legitimacy. What is obviously a love poem may also be understood as metaphysical communion; a You may be understood as a woman, as a child, or as God. Indeed, the closed unity of meaning of a poem is so stringent that it scarcely allows itself to be redefined by a larger context, as is sometimes the case with unities of speech whose true meaning is first provided by the context. With a poem one can certainly focus on the larger context represented by a sequence of poems, and search there for a more widely spanning coherence. This is familiar to hermeneutics, and one can always move into ever larger contexts: the context represented by a volume of poetry composed by the author, the context of his collected work—or at least that of certain phases in his artistic development—or even the context of an age. All of this is correct and widely known at least since Schleiermacher's theory of the hermeneutic circle, which makes our contemporary theorists turn red. Yet none of this weakens the meaning of the concept of coherence.

The stringency of the demand for coherence decreases in this scale, and for good reason. Thus, for example, in the present sequence one clearly sees how Celan "composed": the statement of the introductory poems, the development of the principal theme and the recapitulation of the whole in the finale corresponds to the construction of a musical composition. And yet it would be wrong, in my opinion, to overestimate the value of this unity. It is there, but only on the basis of the self-standing individual configurations of the poems, and only as a loose and secondary assemblage of unity. This is even more true of the poet's collected work. This too is the voice of a human being, no doubt. Unmistakable and unique, a style recognizable even when imitated, though obviously only awkwardly. In the variety of his forms, colors, and motifs, the poet also uses a uniform palette. And yet even the motifs are a matter unto themselves. If, as it is told, Celan once admonished some interpreters of one of his poems for speaking of the "lyrical I" by saying: "But isn't it the lyrical I *of this* poem!"—then I too would like to acknowledge that while research into motifs can sharpen the eye for seeing certain details better, such as what "stone" means in Celan, isn't it the stone *of this* poem? With respect to the legitimate task of studying Celan's poetic vocabulary as such, this must not be forgotten.

It is a different matter when, as emphasized above, the poem itself explicitly refers back to something previously said. This can undoubtedly constitute a significant moment of interpretation, and is quite apparent with Celan, for example in all of his explicit quotations, say, of Hölderlin, or the expressly marked allusions to Brecht. Now it cannot be denied that there are also subliminal allusions which can and should be made evident with some degree of certainty. The boundaries of mere supposition and of associations which remain private are obviously fluid, and the task is endless. In the end it is a question of tact whether or not explicating and elucidating the manifold syntax of connotations, to which such allusions indeed also belong, dissolves or undermines the speech's figure of meaning and the unity of the transpositional movement that represents understanding.

In conclusion must it still be emphasized just how modest the claim of any interpretation is? Conclusive interpretation simply does not exist. Every interpretation seeks only to be an approximation, and would not be what it can be without taking up its historical-effective position *[wirkungsgeschichtlichen Ort]* and thereby entering into the effective event of the work. This does not mean that an interpretation should reject the helpful knowledge which scholarship can contribute. But neither will it be limited to what can be "recognized" with such methods, for to do so would be to refrain from taking up the real challenge of interpretation: to say how one understands. Scholarly assistance in understanding can also not be expected if the posing of a question has not been itself already preceded by the effort to understand. Understanding is not merely the fruit of literary

critical research; it must be present at the beginning and remain decisive throughout.

Every interpretation must strive, of course, for its own re-traction. Just as the poem is a unique utterance, an incomparable and untranslatable balance of sound and meaning upon which reading is built, so the interpreting word also remains a unique utterance. Similarly, its completion cannot be successful without the inner ear "hearing" every word of the interpreted text, and without our considering and following the linguistic movement of the poem constantly bringing us back from the "unnameable" which interpretive thinking imposes, and which Kant's "concept in readiness" *[in Anschlag gebrachten Begriff]* would like to account for. The present attempt continues for a few rounds the play of imagination and understanding *[Verstand]* described by Kant as aesthetic experience (the judgment of taste), by trying to say what it understands and trying to show in the exact text itself that the exegesis is not connected to anything capricious, but rather merely tries to say as accurately as possible what it believes is there.

Epilogue to the Revised Edition

1. What must the reader know?

Paul Celan was a *poeta doctus.* Although he possessed extraordinary technical knowledge in many fields, he did not scorn the use of the lexicon. As I know from personal conversations, he also did not hesitate to reproach mistaken interpreters for having not simply consulted a lexicon. Of course, readers of poetry do not usually work with a lexicon. The poet has always preferred to think that everything needed for understanding his poetry could and should be known. In response to inquiries, Celan often gave a single piece of advice: simply keep reading the poems again and again—and understanding is bound to come.

I followed this procedure from the start as I entered more deeply into the "Breath-crystal" cycle—on the whole, not without some success. In many of Celan's poems, indeed with most of the ones from his late period, I would have had to increase my knowledge first by using scholarly aids. For me that is especially true when it comes to the cultural treasures of the Jewish religious tradition and the mysticism of the Kabbalah, about which I know very little. In these poems, Hebraic or elements of obviously Jewish theological language indicate what the uninitiated must do. Even in the continuation of "Breath-crystal," in *Breath-turn,* I would have been required to expand my knowledge somewhat if I wanted to work through even the primary level of semantics successfully. In choosing "Breath-crystal," I was especially fortunate because I was generally able to find my way without any scholarly aids. I had no lexicon at hand. I lay in a

sand-pit in the Dutch dunes and mulled the verses over, "listening earnestly in the damp wind," until I thought I understood
them. Of course it is an entirely different question to what extent
exegetical words can represent such an encounter without di-
minishing it. A poetic statement will more or less reach anyone
whose ears are open, who does not shut his or her eyes, or stop
thinking. The commentator must try to fathom the details and
mediate between an informed understanding and the reader's
imagination.

Basically, I fully agree with the poet that everything is found
in the text, and that all biographical-occasional moments belong
to the private sphere. Since they are not found in the text, they
do not belong to it. This limits the value of information that comes
from someplace else, say, from friends who have heard something
from the poet. There are certainly cases where such information
can correct an interpretive error that should and could have been
avoided. It is not the poet's fault if a poem is misunderstood—
and certainly not his intention. Understanding a poem correctly
requires one in all cases to completely forget private and occasional information. It just isn't there in the text. All that matters is
understanding what the text itself says, irrespective of any guid-
ance which might be provided by outside information.

Allow me to illustrate this with the example of a well-
known text: "Who, if I cried, would hear me among the angelic
orders?" This is the famous beginning of the *Duino Elegies.*
Someone discovered that this beginning came to Rilke as he
stood by the precipice in Duino in the midst of a stormy day,
looked out onto the churning sea, and listened. Yet even if true,
this information must be immediately forgotten if one wants to
understand what the appeal to the "angels" really means in
Rilke's poetry.

On the other hand, every reader, and especially every commentator, will be utterly thankful when corrected by people who
know something that should and could be known. It is not then
a matter of something private or incidental, but of the elements
of the poetic speech itself. I too have benefited periodically from
various corrections, some useful, some even essential in adjust-
ing something which had been understood inadequately. For
example, it was useful to me to learn the technical meaning of

"penitents' snow" *[Büßerschnee]* from a source of information on mountain climbing, for which I have Mr. Nypels to thank. It convincingly explained the preceding expression "human-shaped snow". It is similarly useful to know that "honey-comb ice" is not a poetic invention, but a precise technical term, or that "temple forceps" should lead one to think about the obstetrician's forceps. All of these are primary semantic determinations of the text *[Textbefunde]*, and it is good to have precise knowledge about them. While they in no way constitute a complete interpretation, they do make a kind of grammatical and semantic contribution toward that end. Whether they have an effect on the interpretation, that is, on the actual statement of the poem, remains to be seen in each individual case.

Let us examine these examples: I am curious, for example, whether in the last poem (page 123) the resonances of my idea of the repenting pilgrim who journeys along the opened path are really completely invalid. As I know now through the mountaineering information, the image of the landscape is not only evoked poetically, but also described quite precisely in the "penitents' snow" of which the poem speaks. Nevertheless, one can still ask why the poet chooses this peculiar technical term here. Those who know the term will understand more precisely why it is previously called "human-formed snow." But is that its only meaning? It cannot be denied that using "human-formed snow" to explain "penitents' snow" or "penitents' snow" to explain "human-formed snow" means more. These explanations allow us to see a whole, namely, that the way toward the "breath-crystal" leads through the dead indifference of human snow. Perhaps one can ask whether the speaker also sees this as a path of repentance, a path which passes through repentance as it is traversed. Atonement is conscious renunciation, and it seems clear to me what sort of renunciation is demanded here. It concerns the sin of the vanity which inflates "the commonly experienced" into false witness. Only that person who renounces the banal effects of intrusive idle chatter, and wanders out past anyone else equally repentant, can ultimately reach the welcoming tables. Is that the way it should perhaps be understood?

Why else does it say "penitents' snow"? One should not resort here to comparative topics. I, too, realize that snow is a polyvalent symbol, that it forms the basis of the entire volume *Snowpart*,* and that it also frames the "Breath-crystal" cycle, in which both the first and last poems speak of snow. I have nothing against topical research. But every poem is its own topos; indeed, its own world, never repeated—as unique as the world itself. Even this penitents' snow is what it is only here. This is in agreement with Celan's Meridian speech.

So I am glad to take up what I have learned, and yet I find in this case that although what I have learned is useful, it does not influence what the poem actually says.

I find this also true of the "temple-forceps" (page 100). In his interesting essay "Mystical Elements in Heidegger and Celan" (*Zeitwende*, 1983), Pöggeler argues that "You and your sleep" refers to the Schechina and her birth.** But one cannot find a single word about that in the poem. On the other hand, Pöggeler's recollection of the obstetrician's forceps is indeed entirely correct. But this concerns simply the most external semantic level. I should have taken this into consideration, but I would have needed to make a correction only if doing so did more than merely amplify what I had already understood about the poem. How does it stand? Which birth does the poem then speak about? Are the obstetrician's forceps used in birth ever eyed by the jugal bone of the newborn? But this is what the poem says. This observation compels one to take "temple-forceps" immediately as a reference to the graying temples, which is what I have done. The text forces one to understand the glance in the mirror, the alarm over the first signs of aging. This grants the ending "it's your birthday" its true, bitter meaning. God knows, this is no birthday joy: aging and death, what remains of your sleep, are celebrating their birthday! The obstetrician's forceps suggested by the temple-forceps anticipate this point, as I now clearly see.

The third example (page 115) mentioned in Pöggeler's essay begins with "armored-ridges" and is a completely different matter. Here the acquired corrections concern an essential point. When I learned of them some years ago, I was immediately persuaded,

---

*The title of Celan's last volume of poetry, *Schneepart*, published in 1970.

**A translation of Pöggeler's essay has appeared in *Word Traces* (Baltimore: Johns Hopkins University Press, 1994), pp. 75–109.

and recognized an essential increase for my understanding of the poem. That is why I looked for a better interpretation than the one originally attempted, and incorporated it into the present text. Indeed, it remains true that the poem plays with the association between the earth's crust and the crust of language. However, it has since become clear to me that I should have taken the verse "your terrain" in the first stanza literally. Here my knowledge was inadequate, and I should have consulted a lexicon, assuming the right advice could have been found there, or acquired the correct explanation from somewhere else (for instance, from friends, as was the case with the "hunger-candles," page 74).

2. Variants

I was very excited about the opportunity of seeing the variants of the poem cycle I had interpreted. The drafts of the poem "Flower" made public by Kurt Bücher at the Paris colloquium on Celan (1979), led me to expect that I could find among Celan's well-ordered papers something like an authentic commentary, as in the case of the Hölderlin variants. Needless to say, the preliminary stages of a definitive version cannot simply be used as incontrovertible evidence for interpretation, since the poet is always free to reject his initial efforts later on. Nevertheless, in the case of "Flower," the yield was great.

Thanks to Beda Allemann, I now have the variants of the poem cycle discussed above. Alas, the yield is modest. The poet seems to have worked out this part of his opus with relatively few sketches and variants. Perhaps my preference for these twenty-four poems has something to do with the poet having been able to follow to an extraordinary degree a single poetic impulse. Moreover, most of the variants are really not genuine sketches of the poems, but traces of work. In what follows, I would like to share and discuss the few variants which are of interest for the interpretation.

Page 70
The preliminary stage of the poem's concluding section sounds very different. After the colon, instead of "whenever I . . . " one finds:

> I come with seven
> leaves from the tribe of the
> seven
>
> ich komme mit sieben
> Blättern vom Sieben-
> stamm.

I do not know what the tribe of seven is. Does it have something to do with the seven-armed cult lamp? The variation only shows us that a genuinely esoteric expression has been replaced in the definitive version by a thoroughly common and accessible connection: the lush growth of the mulberry tree. The only part of the definitive text already anticipated in the sketch seems to be in the repetition "seven leaves from the tribe of seven," which hints at abundance. It almost sounds like a harvest or a trophy. The definitive version has far greater sensuous power, and expresses the resplendent overabundance of this time of sprouting and budding and blossoming which can scarcely be endured.

Page 74

Only one verse in the final draft becomes indirectly a bit clearer from the sketch, namely, verse 6: "with an eye / like yours / on each of my fingers..." reads in the sketch as follows: "(sleepless like you), with your open eye on each of the fingers" [die ich (schlaflos wie du) dein offenes Aug an jedem der Finger]. The parantheses here mean that this piece was immediately deleted by Celan himself. It is interesting because it picks up the reference to "sleepless" in verse 2. Verse 6 speaks of those "bright, eye-like finger tips" [augengleichen hellen Fingerspitzen] whose openness also includes a blindness. "An eye like yours" is thus an open eye which sees nothing, and this is, in fact, meaningful through the reference to "sleepless."

Page 78

The variant "heaven's acid" instead of "heaven's coin" was unequivocally designated by Celan in 1967 as a printing error (see the letter to Dr. Unseld from January, 1968). There is no doubt that "Heaven's coin" was the original version, and the poet set it down again in 1967. In fact, the "grooves" fit only with "heaven's coin" and not with "heaven's acid." But it does appear that for a while the poet himself had a preference for "heaven's acid." The draft to think about reads:

> Into the heaven's coin in the door crack
> You mint the word,
> which I betrayed,
> when with prayinging fists I
> . . .
> the roof over us . . .

> *In die Himmelsmünze im Türspalt*
> *Prägst du das Wort,*
> *das ich verriet,*
> *als ich mit betetenden Fäusten*
> . . .
> *das Dach über uns*

Here the semantic unity of "coin" *[Münze]* and "mint" *[Prägung]* is striking. This was undoubtedly an original and vivid unity. The later change, which also remained definitive, reads:

> Into the grooves
> of heaven's coin in the door crack
> you press the word, from which I unrolled.

> *In die Rillen*
> *der Himmelsmünze im Türspalt*
> *preßt du das Wort, dem ich entrollte . . .*

Here the addition of "into the grooves" *[in die Rillen]* is likewise clearly in agreement with "heaven's coin." In contrast, the replacement of "you mint" *[prägst du]* with "you press" *[preßt du]* leads to a peculiar difficulty. With it, the sense of the image *[Bildvision]* has definitely changed. This may be why "which I betrayed" was changed into the merely vivid and scarcely value laden "from which I unrolled." The origin of the printing error "heaven's acid," as well as the fact that it was overlooked, does remain puzzling. "Heaven's acid" would certainly be the *lectio dificilior.* How did it get into the text? One has to consider whether the poet was responsible, and if not, whether the fact that he could overlook the mistake for such a long time is somehow meaningful. It does seem here that the poet acquired a certain preference for "heaven's acid." This played a role, if not consciously, then at least unconsciously, in the slip of overlooking the error. It appears as if in his increasing gloom and bitterness, Celan remained for a time partial to the idea of corrosive acids which come from heaven in the place of a redemptive blessing—an idea which had always been near to him—until he once again properly corrected the original version. (See *Atemwende* [II, page 38] : "The acids of heaven and earth flow together" *[Himmels- und Erdsäure flossen zusammen].)* That the wrong variant went unnoticed for such a long time is, in any case, hermeneutically interesting. I have acknowledged these subsequent clarifications by not allowing the false version to appear for itself, despite the fact that it remains hermeneutically interesting that the concept of heaven's acid does not seem all that remote.

The printing error is in no way as misleading as the famous case of Hölderlin's "high youth understands, who looks at the world" *[hohe Jugend versteht, wer in die Welt blickt].* For an entire century, "virtue" *[Tugend]* was read instead of "youth" *[Jugend].* In this case, the whole poem is elevated to its taut unity only with the restoration of the authentic text. Reading "virtue" allowed an all too Schillerian rhetorical element to predominate. In our case, however, it cannot hurt when reading the authentic text to have in mind that this heaven from which "I unrolled" has become acidic. The draft, "The word, which I betrayed" (instead of: "from which I unrolled"), also fits well with the denial of heaven and thus the image of "heaven's acid." It sounds like a theology of desperation. —It is also quite interesting that the definitive version speaks of "trembling fists," *[bebenden Fäusten]* and no longer of "praying fists" *[betenden Fäusten].* In fact, the first version has "prayinging" *[betetenden]*, a mistake which actually has the effect of seeming like a first hesitation, a first resistance to the choice of this word—quite a peculiar typographical error. (It is revealing of the tensions at play between meanings that a printing error was preserved in the first edition of this little commentary: although I actually knew nothing of the variants "praying" *[betenden]* and "trembling" *[bebenden]*, the first edition contained "praying"! In apologizing for this printing error, I take the opportunity to point out how lines of meaning spin their threads even behind mistakes.)

Page 83
One draft reads, "I cast the net" *[auswarf]*, and the last two verses are one, namely "with shadows." Both changes are insignificant. However, the use of the imperfect instead of the present tense *[warf* vs. *werf]* gave the earlier text the character of a report. The change in the final version gives the statement a sense of the gnomic and timeless present. The second change "with stone-written shadows" needs no justification other than clarifying the overwhelmingly sensuous beauty which I tried to articulate in my interpretation.

Page 90
Here a draft reads "the decorticated life-floated trunks" *[entrindeten Lebensstämme geflößt]*. While the sensuous precision was greater, there was less conciseness. The change to life-trees (Had Celan thought of Rilke's "O life's trees?" *[O Bäume Lebens]*) permits the loss of life in the decorticated trunks to be perceptible in the expression itself, and with it, the passing of time. In my interpretation I thus would like to emphasize that if the "anti-swimmer" is Time, then at the end Time really does appear in the I itself.

Page 92
Here it is worth following the first stanza in the drafts more precisely:

1. The number, behind which the images jostle
each animated by doom

Die Zahl, hinter der sich die Bilder stauchen
jedes belebt von Verhängnis

2. Draft

The numbers
and the images behind them, with their
doom and anti-
doom
thundering, allayed, agitated

Die Zahlen
und die Bilder dahinter, mit ihrem
Verhängnis und Gegen-
Verhängnis
gewitternd, besänftigt, durchwühlt

If one ignores the last verse, which was apparently replaced
later by the entire second stanza, the two versions are fairly
close. The variants do not tell me very much about the connection between number and time and the connection between time
and consciousness, which becomes clear in the phrase "the images
behind them." The fifth verse "thundering, allayed, agitated,"
however, does not correspond to anything in the second stanza
of the final version. One can only surmise how the back and
forth of time and images, as well as the agitation and calm of
the numbers and images, attest to real inner chaos. Perhaps these
three words in the second draft suggest that the poem's final
words "sings all that" should in fact be heard with a forgiving
and mollifying tone.

Page 95
Instead of "grub," it says "grubbed" *[wühlt]*, that is, the
imperfect. As on page 83, a one-time event is brought into the
gnomic present.

Page 96, verse 9

In the penultimate verse, it says "an eye" *[Ein Aug]*, and then, later deleted by the poet, "over, up—and below" *[über, auf—und nieder]*. I am not sure how these lines stricken by the poet himself should lead the way to my painstakingly interpreted "cut into strips." Had "looking over, up—and below . . ." *[über, auf—und nieder . . . blickend]* been planned? An eye that looks up and down, and in the end oversees the whole, would be an eye that "does justice to all that."

Page 102

Of the variations found in the drafts I will only mention the following:

Verse 7:

"Wishes of worms" *[Wünsche der Würmer]* instead of "conversations of worms." As is so often the case, the final version is more sensuous—less abstract and metaphorical. One literally hears the soft rustling of the worms as a kind of speaking.

Penultimate verse:

"Your arrow-writing whirs" reads "Your (then, deleted: 'legible') arrow-happiness whirs" *[Dein "lesbares" Pfeilglück schwirrt]*. Does this call into question my interpretation of the Archer Death? Shouldn't one understand this "archer" differently, namely as one who shoots unexpectedly and without detection, perhaps even as one who aims to hit the mark of happiness? This phrase in one of the variants would then be harmonious with the other variation, "wishes": wishes and happiness belong together. But in the final draft, so do "conversations" and "arrow-writing." The earlier draft, according to which "arrow-writing" should be "arrow-happiness," namely hitting the mark of what is "legible," would then refer to the success of the poetic word, which holds its ground against ephemerality. In contrast, the final draft makes ephemerality its dominant theme. Thus, I will keep the interpretation of "arrow-writing" in terms of death.

Page 108

In a draft, "The morning-plumb, over-gilded," was "The
(unplumbed) morning" *[Das unauslotbare Morgen]*. The deletion
of the adjective "unplumbed" became "Morning-plumb," which is
a pun. What I attempted to interpret thus appears to undergo a
shift in meaning. The unplumbed morning has a passive meaning, the morning-plumb, in contrast, appears to actively plumb,
and I interpreted it accordingly. The uncertainty of the (never
completely!) plumbable "morning" in my interpretation now
appears to me to come up short. I should have emphasized the
"over-gilded," that is, the questionableness of the day which
proclaims itself with dawn; the poet's last years were completely
cast in this gloom.

In the draft, line 6 uses the imperfect "sticked" *[heftete]*, thus
again the one-time event, which in the final version is elevated
into the gnomic present.

Page 119

One of the drafts begins as follows:

> Word-deposit, under
> the water table,
> which the numberless mob
> of anti-kings in-
> fests with image and copy.

> *Wortaufschüttung, unter*
> *dem Grundwasserspiegel,*
> *den der unzählbare Mob*
> *der Gegenkönige ver-*
> *seucht mit Abbild und Nachbild.*

The draft is undoubtedly much less sensually vivid. To explain
the final version, I would only point to the replacement of "anti-
kings" with "anti-creatures," which makes the uprising of the
mob against the true kings and kingly progeny even clearer.

3. Hermeneutic method?

There is no hermeneutic method. All the methods developed by scholarship can be hermeneutically profitable—if one uses them correctly and does not forget that a poem is not a fact which can be explained as an instance of something more general, the way that an experimentally valid fact is an instance of the law of nature.

Further, a poem cannot be produced by a machine. That a computer can fabricate poems electronically, as Max Bense has demonstrated, is only a false objection. It may be true that a poem can eventually be brought about after infinite combinations of letters. But what matters is that it becomes a poem only when read out of all the computer garbage—and the computer cannot do this too, and even if it does, the computer does not label it a poem, but at most, a grammatically correct speech.

Hermeneutics means not so much a procedure as the attitude of a person who wants to understand someone else, or who wants to understand a linguistic expression as a reader or listener. But this always means: understanding *this* person, *this* text. An interpreter who really has mastered scholary methods uses them only so that the experience of the poem becomes possible through better understanding. He or she will not blindly exploit the text in order to apply a method.

And yet a number of objections have sought to characterize my attempt at interpretation as "hermeneutic," or some other such thing. Those who claim, for example, that all of Celan's poetry, as well as his tragic life, constitutes a single confession and expression of horror about the Holocaust are indeed essentially correct. There are confirmations of this in the Meridian speech, which also alludes to Adorno's related comments. There Celan maintains that contemporary poetry exhibits a powerful tendency toward silence— or that it also no longer suffices to think Mallarmé through to the end. The position at the margins, which Celan ascribes to contemporary poetry, certainly deserves the utmost reflection. But it does not provide us with a principle for understanding his poems better. This is true even for those poems which, like "Death Fugue," are expressly and unambiguously about the Holocaust.

Poetry always remains more—much more—than what even the most committed reader knows beforehand. Otherwise, it would be superfluous.

Another objection is that my procedure is too phenomenological since the poet takes his orientation from word-play to a far greater degree than I am prepared to accept. (Bollack reproached me for this.) This does not make much sense to me. For what is the opposite of "phenomenological"? That words are simply words? That words should make one think of nothing? Or that one is entitled to think of something only with respect to certain words, but not with respect to the poem's overall unity of meaning? A response to this would be that words never have meaning for themselves, and that only through their perhaps polyvalent significance do they construct the one meaning which in the concatenation of resounding lines of meaning nevertheless preserves the unity of the text—and speech as a whole. Or should it be that in understanding such texts, one should not vividly imagine anything? As if words, like concepts, would not be empty without contemplation [Anschauung]. No word has meaning without its context. Even individual words which stand for themselves—like the title word "breath-turn"—first acquire their meaning in context. Thus it must be observed here explicitly that as the title of this volume of poetry, "breath-turn" designates the silent, whisper-like transition and alternation of inhaling and exhaling, whereby the "breath-crystal" of the poem emerges in pure form like a single snowflake. I believe this is what the context of "Breath-crystal," and especially the final poem, teaches. In the Büchner speech, however, "breath-turn" refers, first of all, to a different aspect of the word's significance, namely, the reversal which takes place between inhaling and exhaling, and not primarily the miracle of its imperceptibility. Yet here I would like to ask if a connection exists between both accentuations of the word "breath-turn." Is it not the case that true reversal is never a spectacular occurrence, that it consists rather of a thousand silent imperceptibilities? That would fit very well with the passage in the Meridian speech which says: "Poetry, that can mean a 'breath-turn.' Who knows? Perhaps poetry goes the distance—for art, as well—for the sake of such a breath-turn?"

Pöggeler formulates another objection when he asks if my effort "to reduce Celan's images like Goethe's symbols to generally comprehensible experiences does not fail to recognize that the bold understanding of allegory has been constructed gradually out of incomprensibility through tradition and artifice." In this nice formulation I recognize my own effort! But I would not want to see it sharpened into the opposition between symbol and allegory which, though sanctioned by Goethe, was certainly never practiced. Pöggeler even suggests in this context that I myself—in the tradition of Benjamin—have contributed to the vindication of allegory. But I do not understand why Pöggeler here belabors the opposition between symbol and allegory. In the description of the hazardous enterprise of understanding, I would see primarily nothing more than the fact that we all still know far too little. This is my own deficiency most of all. I wish I were as learned as Pöggeler, and no doubt Pöggeler wishes he were as learned as Celan. As for Celan? Well, certainly he would wish nothing else but to succeed in writing his poem.

It is difficult for me to accept the concept of allegory here at all. I believe Celan would not have sanctioned it any more than the concept of metaphor. If classical antiquity and Christianity were integrated in literate society during the age of the Baroque, that is no longer true today. The cultivated society which would already possess Celan's enormous knowledge simply does not exist. His poetry certainly does not intend to call upon such a cultivated society, one whose knowledge could reach from Homer and the Bible all the way to the Kabbala. Celan wishes to be heard, and he allows for the fact that in the din of modern life, the quiet voice of what is barely understandable is needed to compel patient listening and ultimately raise into consciousness "facts" we ought not to forget. In this sense, the poem which must be written today seeks to be an "irrefutable witness"—but only as a poem. At all times, wherever we are, we will naturally perceive gaps in our knowledge which must be filled. After a few of these have been filled successfully, my question is how one understands what the text itself says. I believe Celan was a genuine poet who journeyed painstakingly and frugally, perhaps even repentantly, to the breath-crystal. And what he sought to discover is the word common to all. Celan had a reason for saying what was quoted above: "simply keep reading the poems again and again—and understanding is bound to come." Obviously he counted on his poems being accessible through general human experience, into which the horrors of our era have entered, as well as through knowledge more or less acquired by all those not closed off to such things. Whether to use any method, or none at all: this would hardly have disturbed him. For it is also undeniably true that although no one can honestly claim to have understood all of his poems completely—in contrast to the way, say, Goethe, can be understood these days—this hermetic poet is nevertheless read by thousands because they respond to his work as poetry. The more precise understanding may be vague and limited, even so, it is understood as poetry. No, allegory presupposes a self-evident consensus which no longer exists today. Poetry today presupposes a consensus which has yet to arise. What I undertook in my investigations with respect to this question was concerned precisely with calling into question the elaborate rending of allegory and symbol. Even in the case of Celan, I believe I follow my own insights.

And so once again, in conclusion: What must the reader know? That both the reader and the interpreter, in this case me, should know as much as possible, and yet still not enough—this seems to me beyond question. Now, central to the basic principle of scholarship is that it can set no borders. Naturally scholarship cannot help but apply all of its methods, including the most current ones. But this does not answer the question of what the reader must know, even with respect to Celan's poems. Poems are not written for scholarship, even when the reader for whom they are written makes use of the aid provided by it. If there is something the reader does not know, he or she can use a lexicon—although these are only the rotten fruits of scholarship. Yet there is another answer to the question of what the reader must know, one that is precise and binding, though incapable of being fixed or regulated. It suggests that the reader must know only as much as he or she needs and can sustain. The reader must know only as much as he or she really can and must bring into the reading or hearing of the poem; only as much as his or her poetic ear can bear without going deaf. This is often only a little, but even so, it is still more than when it is too much.

There is a Socratic saying which I would like to apply here to the gold of scholarship. At the end of *Phaedrus*, Socrates prays to Pan, who had presided over the summery hour of conversation, and requests, among other things: "as much gold as a reasonable person can carry with him." The gold of scholarship is indeed gold. Like all gold, it must be used properly. This is particularly true when applying scholarship to the experience of art. The hermeneutical principle here is this: an interpretation is correct only when it is finally able to disappear completely, having entered completely into a new experience of the poem. Especially with Celan, we rarely reach this point.

Meaning and Concealment of Meaning in Paul Celan

M eaning and concealment of meaning in the poetry of Paul Celan—with this theme we do not actually legitimize a particular perspective from which to guide the interpretation of Celan's art, but rather simply articulate what anyone experiences upon becoming acquainted with Celan's work. One feels the attraction of a precise meaning while also being aware that this meaning is withheld, perhaps even deliberately concealed. What is behind this style of poetry, one typical not only of Celan, but indeed of an entire generation, and how do we deal with it?—these are the questions we must ask ourselves. Addressing the former does not require us to pose theoretical considerations; it requires us to read.

Perhaps to begin a general observation will suffice. Contemporary poetry seems to strive to permit the gravitational pull of words to operate fully without constraining them by means of logic and syntax. This blocklike speech, in which the individual words that stimulate impressions are situated next to each other, does not mean that words cannot be conjoined in the unity of an intention of meaning. But the accomplishment of this is a challenge left to the reader. It is by no means the case that the poet arbitrarily conceals and obscures the unity of meaning. This is precisely how the poet seeks to reveal something. Through the blocklike assemblage the poet releases the multidimensionality of the associations of meaning which is suppressed by the practical unity of intention in logically controlled, one-dimensional everyday speech. It is a mistake to think that because the semantic associations are not unambiguous one can understand nothing of the poem. Moreover, it is a mistake to think that the unity of speech-intention is missing. That is what makes the poem.

The poem reads:

TENEBRAE

We are near, Lord,
near and graspable.

Grasped already, Lord,
clutching one another, as if
the body of each of us were
your body, Lord.

Pray, Lord,
pray to us,
we are near.

Wind-awry we went there,
we went there to bend
over hollow and ditch.

To the watering-hole we went, Lord.

It was blood, it was,
what you poured out, Lord.

It glistened.

It cast your image into our eyes, Lord,
Eyes and mouth stand so open and empty, Lord.

We have drunk, Lord.
The blood and the image that was in the blood, Lord.

Pray, Lord.
We are near.

TENEBRAE

Nah sind wir, Herr,
nahe und greifbar.

Gegriffen schon, Herr,
ineinander verkrallt, als wär
der Leib eines jeden von uns
dein Leib, Herr.

Bete, Herr.
bete zu uns,
wir sind nah.

Windschief gingen wir hin,
gingen wir hin, uns zu bücken
nach Mulde und Maar.

Zur Tränke gingen wir, Herr.

Es war Blut, es war,
was du vergossen, Herr.

Es glänzte.

Es warf uns dein Bild in die Augen, Herr,
Augen und Mund stehn so offen und leer, Herr.
Wir haben getrunken, Herr.
Das Blut und das Bild, das im Blut war, Herr.

Bete, Herr.
Wir sind nah.

As always with titles which have a specific meaning, the title "Tenebrae" gives rise to a preconception. One must obviously recognize that Tenebrae means not only eclipse, but a specific eclipse, namely, the one which, according to the Gospel, took place when Jesus expelled his last breath on the cross. In Catholic ritual this is celebrated as the Passion-matin, or Good Friday matin, so as to ritually repeat the event of the heavenly eclipse at the moment of Jesus' death. This rite of the Passion-matin also includes a reading of the "Lamentations of Jeremiah." The word of Jesus on the cross, "My God, my God, why hast thou forsaken me," is itself a quotation from the Old Testament. In this way Catholic ritual already conjoins the God-forsakenness that was the fate of the Jewish people in their Babylonian exile with the God-forsakenness of Jesus on the cross. But doesn't the evocation of this heavenly eclipse by the contemporary poet extend further? Shouldn't one think about the suffering and dying of the Jews in Hitler's concentration camps? Or ultimately about the universal human fear of death? About God's rage, how in the Jewish history of the Old Testament he punishes his chosen people? Or about the impiousness that has emerged in this age of the slackening of the Christian traditions? All of this resonates in the single word "Tenebrae" and permits us to listen.

In what sense then does the poem connect up to these "Tenebrae"? One thing is certain: the poem is not called "Tenebrae" without evoking the entire tradition of the passion story—from the Old Testament lamentations through the passion story on up to the passion of human beings under the darkened heaven of our present time. This is a preliminary orientation point which must attain a more precise exposition grounded in the poem itself.

The poem is a provocation. Should it be understood as a blasphemous poem or as a Christian poem? Is it not blasphemous for the poem to say unequivocally to the dying Jesus: you should pray not to God, who has forsaken you, but to us? The meaning of this opposition is unmistakable: because God does not know death; at the hour of death He is unreachable. But because we do know death, know about it and its inescapability, we understand this last cry of forsakenness all too well. Obviously Jesus' last words were not meant to express doubt about his God, but rather to attest to the overwhelming power of suffering and of death. Therein lies a last commonality [Gemeinigkeit] between the son of man and the children of man: both endure death.

But what does it mean that Jesus should prefer to pray to us? Is that an extreme mockery and rejection of faith in God and prayer to God, not to mention a brazen, impious distortion of the entire passion story and the forsakenness of Jesus on the cross?— And yet is this last forsakenness not a crucial moment in the Christian doctrine of incarnation itself, so that the poet so to speak approaches the actual sense of Christian doctrine in its concept of Jesus' representative suffering and dying? I do not intend to try answering this question, since it cannot be answered. It is not the poet's opinion that matters, but rather what is expressed in the poem. And that has been left open by the poet. As with all the language configurations created by the poet, it is necessary for us to decide for ourselves. We cannot rely on him.

In any case, Jesus is exhorted to pray to us. What does it mean here "to pray"? What does praying mean? The poem begins unambiguously with the provocation: "Pray to us, Lord." This alludes to Jesus' last words on the cross: "My God, my God, why hast thou forsaken me?" Is that even a prayer? Certainly it is an appeal to God. And perhaps it really can be said that making such an appeal is precisely what constitutes the only possible content of a prayer. For "we do not know what we should pray" (as suggested in the Epistle to the Romans and Bach's famous motet). In fact, praying cannot mean asking for something. As if we could even know by ourselves what is right for us. Rather the granting of the prayer appears to precede any fulfillment of possible wishes. The granting of the prayer is itself the prayer's being-heard, the existence [Dasein] of he to whom one calls in the prayer. That he hears and that one is thereby not forsaken— this is the granting. So understood, the content of Jesus' last words is prayer itself, the last cry imploring to be by me, imploring not to leave me alone.

Yet for every person the hour of death, this last rebellion of Nature in us, is the hour of one's utmost forsakenness. The brazen turn taken by the poem consists precisely in the fact that it concerns not only God's forsakenness, but the forsakenness of all other human beings. What does it mean to pray to these human beings? As if human beings could offer any assistance here! However if "praying" means calling in such a way that the other hears, then a deeper meaning emerges: since human beings know death, since they stand under the law of death, they are in unique solidarity with the dying. This is what the dying should ascertain by praying to us, this last commonality.

This commonality is established in the poem's introduction, and stands at the beginning and the end of this introduction, as well as the poem's conclusion: we are near. "We are near, Lord, near and graspable." To my mind, the "we" has a soft tone. Not you are near, but we. This is anything but an imitation of Hölderlin. The same sound with which the "Patmos" hymn begins: "God is near, but difficult to hold",* goes in the complete opposite direction. It is not that God is near for us, but that we are near for the Lord. The transition from "graspable" to "already grasped" sets up a climax leading to "clutched and clutching" together. It negates the distance between the grasper and the grasped, the separateness of the dying from those still alive.

For what are we grasped by? Certainly not by you, Lord, for whom we are named graspable. What we are grasped by can only be the "absolute Lord"—death—to whom human beings belong. He is indeed our lord to such a degree that before him we are all equal. "Clutching one another," we hold ourselves as if groping around in the throes of death. Such despair is so much our true commonality that human beings, clutching one another, seek aid and salvation in every one else: "as if the body of each of us were your body, Lord."

As the poem continues it becomes completely clear that "your body" refers here unambiguously to the body of the dying and dead Jesus. Yet the phrase also refers to something else. It seems significant to me that it says "the body of each of us" and not: "our body," the body of us all. Each of us is for each other a fellow creature [der Nächste] whom we nevertheless cannot reach. For in dying each of us is as alone and forsaken as Jesus dying on the cross. The experience of death is isolating, as

---

*"Nah ist, doch schwer zufassen, der Gott."

Heidegger suggests in his concept of the *Jemeingkeit** of death, or as Rilke speaks about it in well-known poems. Clearly the suggestion is that death, which is so horribly isolating, unites everyone with each other, as well as with the dying Jesus. It is being clutched in the inescapability of death itself. This is certainly the conclusion pronounced by the poem: "Pray, Lord, pray to us, we are near." One with you in the *Jemeingkeit* of dying, this being-one also represents unity and closeness even in the most extreme forsakenness.

This commonality between Jesus and us, that we belong to death, is not simply pronounced. Indeed, it is told as a story, and if I am right, at the end we see not only the inescapability of death, but also an acceptance of death. That is not to say that anything even hints at the Christian overcoming of death through the Resurrection and the belief in it. There is no word of that here. The acceptance of death consists rather in drinking your blood and "the image in your blood." This is again a thoroughly un-Christian "communion." It sounds as if he had died "ahead" of us, and that when we die after him, we will accept the same forsakenness, the same darkness of God. In this sense he appears to have died for us.

The poem unfolds the meaning of this fearful closeness and paradoxical unity in that it seemingly goes back in time—not into a historical time, but into an eternally recurring time, the time of any given human existence *[Dasein]*. The story reports the way in which we became aware of our unity with the dying Jesus. The imperfect tense already shows that our prehistory is also being told, a prehistory that always already lies behind us. "Wind-awry we went there." The expression "wind-awry" suggests a lack of orientation, a lack of direction. The hopelessness of human life, the path of which is the desire to avoid dying, is therein compressed into a single word. "Wind-awry we went there, we went there, to bend over hollow and ditch." The repetition of "we went there" makes vivid the permanence, the

---

*Heidegger's untranslatable neologism *"Jemeinigkeit"* combines the term for "commonality" *[Gemeinigkeit]* with the adverb "je," which serves as a compound element of the German terms for "each," "anyone," and related terms *[jeder, jemand]*.

stubborn persistence of those who go here, in other words, the stubborness of our will to live. "Hollow and ditch" naturally evoke moisture, water, which might quench the thirst that drives us, thereby evoking thirst itself. Quenching the thirst for life could almost be the formal structure of life as such. This is indeed how the words "we go to the watering-hole, Lord" are to be understood. It is the animal-natural element of our will to live which drives us as it does the animals—hence "to the watering-hole." But the meaning of these words immediately lapses into paradox.

For what is described here? Ultimately, the path in which the living hope to live away from death. The paradox is this: the only drink we find is blood, and that means the path itself leads us now to confront the very thing it drives us away from, namely death. Once again an emphatic utterance is employed. "It was blood, it was . . . " suggests above all the sheer horror. Instead of water it is blood—and yet that is what the "watering-hole" becomes when first we have learned to recognize and acknowledge in Jesus' death on the cross the inescapability of death.

The first step toward this knowledge is pronounced in the verses "it was,/what you poured out, Lord./It glistened." These verses have tremendous sensory power. They evoke the peculiar glistening of spilled blood, which contains something ghastly about it. This is not the glistening of transfiguration. Much more remarkable is the fact that no promise is tied up in it; it does not say "poured out for us." Of course what is in this way not said is not simply absent. It does resonate and thereby acquires a new presence: namely that of withdrawal and refusal. Thus it "means" us, but in a seemingly completely different sense than that of representative suffering. For this blood mirrors nothing but death itself, Jesus' corpse. That is why the poem further intensifies the horrifying reality which this death holds for those driven by the thirst for life: "It cast your image into our eyes, Lord,/Eyes and mouth stand so open and empty, Lord." This is the utter uncanniness of death, the horrifying strangeness that for the living cuts off the dying into utter oblivion, the strangeness that here confronts those driven by the thirst for life, who are on the lookout for a drink. The theme of the Pietà can be heard.

But the fact that this image we are bending over is in blood tells us still more. What confronts us as the crucified man mirrored in blood is indeed our own condition of being marked by death. In it we encounter ourselves, shudder at our own self-forgetting, take fright at ourselves. "As if/the body of each of us were/your body, Lord." Indeed the blood and the image contained in it is the drink itself. That is the great affirmative conclusion with which the poem completes its argument: "We have drunk, Lord./The blood and the image that was in the blood, Lord." In other words: although it was blood, the blood in which the dead Jesus was mirrored, we have drunk it. We have accepted it and not rejected it in fright. We have accepted that we must die. That is what gives us the right to say: "Pray, Lord, we are near."

With that the poem is complete. Observing ourselves in the certainty of our death, we experience a last unity with the dying Jesus, who feels abandoned by God. In concluding, one must thus again observe that in the tradition of the evangelists, Jesus' outcry of forsakenness is not meant to express a slackening of his readiness for sacrifice or any doubt about his God. The "Yet not as I will, but as Thou wilt" is in no way contradicted by this last outcry. To the contrary. What first completes God's transformation into man is that the dying Jesus feels God has forsaken him. That is truly human. And it confirms that dying is not in any way easier for Jesus. Even if the Christ believes that Jesus is God, it does not mean that he has not really suffered death. The biblical account suggests rather that Jesus has borne his martydom until the very last moment, and it is precisely this martyrdom upon which our unity with him and our closeness to him rests.

Thus I raise anew our opening question. Is this blasphemy? Even if one must guard against ascribing to the poetic statement a false unambiguousness one still must admit that the aspect of the blasphemous presented by the whole is nonetheless transformed into its virtual opposite. It is indeed truly a decisive departure from Christian tradition when it says: "Pray not to God, but pray to us." But it remains an act of piety—having to pray—to which Jesus is exhorted. What the poem articulates is an admission of human helplessness and hopelessness with respect to the incomprehensibility of death. Christian elements thus resonate even in withdrawal and absence. In the continually repeated "Lord" the voice which speaks for us formally acknowledges that the dying Jesus on the cross remains our Lord, as one who suffers and who is forsaken, if not as the Christ of the Resurrection.

Thus while Celan's invocation of the Tenebrae is not simply a reiteration or acceptance of Christianity's message, it is even less a mockery or derision of faith. It is an affirmation of distress. By taking death seriously and accepting it as the destiny of human beings beyond all hope and comfort, the poem approaches the ultimate intention of the Christian doctrine of the incarnation, with which Christianity rises above the other known world religions: no God who is not human, no God who does not bear dying upon himself, can provide hope and redemption for the faithful. The poem does not articulate the overcoming of death as it is promised in Christianity, and yet Jesus, bearing death upon himself, remains the "Lord."

At the end of this interpretive effort it may be possible to specify more precisely the nature of the concealment of meaning inherent in this kind of poetry. Our reading of the poem has demonstrated that it is not a deliberate concealment and obfuscation of a given meaning which might be clearly and unambiguously stated. The poet here has entered into a sphere which possesses its own distinguishing constellations. The extreme moment of the "suffering and dying of our Lord Jesus," his last breath on the cross, is fused together with the fear of death and the certainty of death, a power both hidden and present in each of us, and it is this mysterious unity to which the poem attests through its own compelling endurance.[1]

Obviously, the framework of these verses, which must withstand such tensions, cannot be viewed from the perspective of the stylistic ideal characteristic of our literary tradition since Goethe, namely Goethe's "naturalness" [Natürlichkeit]. As if by themselves, Goethe's rhymes and verses are ordered by an incomparable naturalness and simplicity. They flash up like brilliantly wrought jewelry, and yet seem utterly natural. This is the standard by which we continue to measure poetic craft and art, but so doing ignores the fact that the situation of the German language Goethe inherited was completely different. At the time German had yet to wrest its versatility and expressibility from the opposing forces of Latin-humanistic ornateness and French-oriented linguistic norms. The incredible impact of Goethe's early work was founded on his ability to achieve this with an ease we find incomprehensible. But in the context of his time what Goethe dared was an often astonishing poetic boldness, especially with works such as "Pandora's Return" or even the "West-Eastern Divan," which by no means found immediate acceptance.

Even more significant in this regard is the example of Hölderlin, who found a completely new kind of lyric for a completely new message. He stands at the dawn of the twentieth century, and indeed was recognized only then. During his own time, Hölderlin's great hymns were not even regarded as the poetic creations of a sane mind, but rather as the product of the insanity that later befell him. His romantic allies dared to publish only portions of these writings, though to be sure, only because they themselves had never dared such bold poetic expression. Thus Hölderlin's poems were brought to contemporary readers only in fragmented form, and remained so through the early part of this century. In 1914 the definitive volume of Hellingrath's Hölderlin edition appeared in which for the first time Hölderlin's late hymns were presented to the public so fully decoded and critically reviewed that contemporaries suddenly recognized them as great poetry. The discovery of Hölderlin's late work in our own century was epoch-making because it enabled subsequent innovations in language and poetic risks in the manner of Trakl, the late Rilke, or even the Celan we are considering here. For Hölderlin's late poetry, this blocklike utterance derived from the style of Pindar's odes, suddenly emerged as a remarkably calculated, conscious, and demanding poetic form. To ascribe it to the dissolution of language brought on by Hölderlin's madness was an error we cannot even comprehend today; even among the very latest of the poems from the period of his madness, we observe today a form of indescribable beauty.[2] It simply demonstrates that poetic language often makes impossible demands. All modes of speaking are not poetically conceivable at all times.

Today there is also the experience that poetry is no longer "welcome," since the conventions of language of our time demand other stimuli. This is important to bear in mind in evaluating the poetic style of our age. As the Russian formalists already recognized, there are laws for the diminishment as well as the intensification of stimulus through contrast. Thus the new mass rhetoric, which has made inroads in our society through the mass media, has contributed to the affinity of poetic and especially lyric language for the hermeticism that characterizes our epoch. How can language configurations be stabilized today so that we can return to them, and so that the more we do so, the more meaningful they become and the more they can respond to our questions? To stabilize language configurations today so as to prevent them from vanishing into the floods of informational chatter that wash over us clearly requires entirely different, sharper provocations and forms of resistance than were needed in, say, Goethe's time. Thus hermetic poetry's concealment of meaning may come across as an artificial encumbrance. Yet it also serves as a bulwark against dispersion into the faint oscillation of the tuned-in loudspeaker. It is a matter of summoning up something to show the poetic configuration in action and to withdraw from the prosification that is levelling everything.

Celan gave it his utmost. And so he demands nothing less, and often more than we can muster.

Gadamer's Notes

1. See also the interpretation of the poem in the context of my essay "Der Tod als Frage" (*Gesammelte Werke*, Volume 4, pp. 161–172).

2. See my *Laudatio* to Roman Jakobson in R. Jakobson, H.-G. Gadamer, and E. Holenstein, *Das Erbe Hegels, II.* Frankfurt: Suhrkamp, 1984.

A Phenomenological
and Semantic Approach
to Celan?

As a participant in the Heidelberg Celan Colloquium, I found
myself in the role of reader and admirer.* In that circle of
Germanists, who applied scholarly methods in approach-
ing this difficult poet, I remained the outsider, aspiring merely to
reconstruct again and again the texts of poems which move and
speak to me. This is not the task of scholarly analysis, but it
remains the ultimate point of any scholarly concern with art. Now
it must be said that because of its artistic obscurities and multifaceted allusions and word-plays, mastering the difficulties of Celan's
late work, which includes "Breath-crystal," demands exacting consideration as well as the application of scholarly methods and
information.

Nevertheless, one should not forget that readers are concerned with the poem, the text, in front of them. That is true of
anyone's association with the work of even this poet. Accordingly,

---

*A Paul Celan Colloquium was held at Heidelberg in 1987. Papers from that
colloquium are published in *Paul Celan "Atemwende": Materialien*, ed.
Gerhard Buhr and Roland Reuss (Würzburg: Königshausen & Neumann,
1991).

Celan. "I cannot make things completely visible"

I do not subscribe here to anything like a "hermeneutical method."
In fact, I really don't know what such a method would be. I seek
only to bring to light what every reader basically does. Similarly,
I do not prefer, say, a phenomenological rather than semantic
method. Certainly, it can hardly be denied that the semantic side
of a Celan text is especially important. Paul Celan himself once
explicitly referred to the polyvalence of his poetic vocabulary:
"The polyvalence of expression takes into account the circumstance that with respect to anything, we observe facets which
make it visible from various angles of sight, various refractions and
dispersions which are not mere appearance. I strive to reproduce
at least linguistically sections from this spectral analysis of things,
to make them visible simultaneously in various aspects and in
permeations with other things that are related, subordinate,
or contrary. For, unfortunately, I cannot make things completely
visible."

Here I must obviously ask: really? Is that not exactly what
the poet can do? The poem itself always unifies the whole.
Despite its manifold references—no, precisely because of them—
the poem creates a many-sided poetic present. For this reason,
it is clear that Celan needed a polyvalent and broken semantics
of bold syncretisms and playful assemblages. What matters is
leaving behind the one-sided pragmatism of familiar, everyday
speech, and, beyond that, giving up certain rhetoric for the sake
of the poeticization. This is the new kind of poetry which characterizes "Breath-crystal." It is a question of making sure that the
poem does not become a "noem."

It is even less meaningful to ascribe a hermeneutical method
to the reader or interpreter who understands. Such a term merely
means that as a reader, one follows the language used to make
something appear. What language shows and makes visible—the
"phenomena"—must be constructed within itself. As an interpreter one must of course isolate the semantic means by which
this showing occurs, but only in order to shift it back again
within the unity of the speech. Even the so-called polyvalence
of words is determined, as in all verbal significance, by the unity
of meaning suggested by the speech as a whole. The unity of
a poem is based on it. Here again I can call upon Celan himself,
who confronts the subject directly in the Meridian address when

he says that it can never be a question of the topos "stone," but rather always only a particular stone in a particular poem. The ultimate task of every reader is thus to make a text speak again. One ought not think this means that the very refined and reflective sense of poesie which Celan attempted to characterize in the Meridian speech as his particular goal invalidates this task, or perhaps makes it even impossible. Reading always means allowing something to speak. The pale, mute signs need articulation and intonation in order to say what they want to say. One ought not be misled here by the grammatology of Jacques Derrida, which elevates "écriture" as the model of undecidable ambiguity. With Celan, it is the ambiguity of words themselves, these voice-traces of meaning. Reading always means letting the sound and meaning of the text arise. There is no way to bypass this basic phenomenon of allowing the text to speak, this basic structure [Grundstruktur] of the unity of meaning in speech.

Therefore in any analysis of semantic polyvalence, the task consists of connecting the subordination of semantic associations with the norm of unity in "listening." To give a well-known example—the first poem of "Breath-crystal" allows for the following semantic analysis: the poem speaks of a mulberry tree and, at the end, the newest leaf on this mulberry tree "shrieks." One can thus take the word mulberry tree [Maulbeerbaum] from the start as simply an allegorical designation for the loudmouthed screaming which disturbs and drowns out the stillness of careful listening. But to do so is to overlook the sensuous appearance which the poem itself is able to conjure up with its words, namely this inexhaustibly sprouting "mulberry tree"—incidentally, not one of Celan's clever neologisms, but a commonly used German term. This mulberry tree thus symbolizes an uncontrollable, inexhaustible germinating power. This is what one must see and what the poem evokes, so that one can say through the course of the poem what the striding amid mulberry trees expresses. One must first see in order to then understand, undertaking a transposition which, through reading again and again, is finally completed as an *understanding of the praise of silence.*

What might be termed the songfulness [Sangbarkeit] of a poem depends on this kind of completion. It is not actual singing. Rather, it is more like meditating—though this is also like song. One can really complete a song only by joining in. Similarly, one can also experience a poem only as its own kind of song, only by allowing its completion to be expressed jointly through speaking. It would be wrong to see this requirement limited by the claim that the strangely corrupt constructions in Celan's texts have no meaning in this sense because blatant tensions, contradictions, breaks, and lapses of coherence appear in the text itself. This is indeed the case, and that is why it is necessary to complete and to understand what the poem wants to say. Such meaning is not the goal of abstract totality, but the unalterable demand that anything written make sense, especially true for a text that is intended as a poetic statement.

Yet I do not want to repeat any of my own interpretations here, nor can I go into detail about individual contributions to the colloquium. That is really not my concern— as long as one grants me the general presupposition that a poet reveals his poetic world only through his art. If so, scholarly analysis might well then focus on the artistic devices themselves, working by means of comparison and separation and with every sort of method, information, and resonance. But all this is still for the sake of producing a more highly articulated level of understanding.

It would be an entirely different task to enter then into the poetics of the Meridian speech, as Buhr has done in a worthwhile study that has much to offer. But it would be a mistake to suppose that the elementary truth that one must make the text speak if one wants to understand it might be somehow addressed in the thematic of the Meridian speech. Of course, the Meridian speech as a whole constitutes an aesthetics of lyric poetry which brings into play the question of Paul Celan's relationship to his great poetic predecessors. However, whether one is reading a text from Goethe or Hölderlin, Mallarmé or Celan, the task of reading remains the same. That is why I myself must admit to understanding only a few selected examples from Celan's late work, by which is meant being able to penetrate them in such a way as to complete them in their natural significative coherence.

Here I cautiously recall the example of Rilke's *Duino Elegies*, which were so unusual for their time that they were subject to countless distorting interpretations and reputed to be dark and incomprehensible. According to Kippenberg, Rilke once read one of these elegies in Leipzig in such a manner that everyone present found it simple, clear, and fully comprehensible. Reading correctly is difficult. It demands that one has achieved correct understanding.

However, what "correct" means here is always relative. Provided he even has the ability, the poet himself will read his own poems differently each time. Reading correctly only means that the text is completable in terms of its own composition and the significative density in all its parts. Allow me once again to consider an example from "Breath-crystal" in order to illustrate the meaning of "correct"—not only the unambiguous meaning of the criterion that applies here, but also the relative character of that criterion. I choose a poem which I already have looked at often, the one in which the expression "my-poem" *[das Mein-Gedicht]* occurs.* Some interpreters still believe that what is meant here is not an analogous form of "false oath" *[Meineid]*, but rather the nothingness of the "so-called" poem which is mine in that it remains private. And yet it must be admitted that only when one hears the analogy to a false oath does the conclusion of the poem, the "irrefutable witness," really "sit" since it recalls the false witness of the "noem." One should not console oneself with the polyvalence theory by assuming that both meanings might be intended, perhaps even citing the enjambment which separates "my" from "poem" as a sign that the "my" is also supposed to convey the sense of privacy. By chance I happened to be in Paris with Celan when this mistaken interpretation—I think it was in an English publication—made him very angry. Naturally, he immediately called upon "irrefutable witness."

I have chosen this example with care. Here one sees that the poem might retain its expression even when one falsely understands what "my-poem" means. But then it would be an inferior poem. Perhaps one could say that it would be keeping with Celan's style to introduce such a word-play. This evasion doesn't help. The monumental conclusion "irrefutable witness" would be without internal support if the false witness of

---

*Gadamer is referring to the last poem in the cycle, "Corroded," page 74 of the present volume.

"my-poem" at the beginning of the text was not there to offer
it. The unity of the expression would be weakened. That is the
criterion unique to poetic speech, undoubtedly relative and variable, as is shown by any variation in intonation. With Celan,
even the line breaks set down in the printed text were variable
when he gave public readings. Of course, the completion of the
unity of meaning when reproduced in speaking can allow or
even demand such variance. Here one might object: "What kind
of a criterion is that supposed to be? It has no demonstrative
force"—in which case I would answer: indeed poems are not
mathematical problems. Ultimately only the completion of meaning, the completion of meaning which puts itself to the test, can
be convincing—for oneself, as well as for anyone else who tries.
Therefore in every discussion about possible interpretations one
must try out the opinions of others if one is ultimately to hear
what is there in the text, the irrefutable witness.

Since so much time has passed since the Heidelberg conference on Celan's "Breath-crystal," I cannot remember in detail
what I myself contributed at the time. My contribution came
entirely out of the situation for which it was intended. Since then
a preponderance of material has been presented against the
studies presented there. I lack the impartiality to render an account of what this tremendous concentration of work and scholarly research means for me as a reader today. This is especially
true in my case since the concentration on the poem cycle
"Breath-crystal" refers back to my own interpretive efforts two
decades ago. It lies in the nature of the subject matter that such
an effort would challenge a younger generation to work on their
own interpretation of this cryptic poetry, using my first attempt
as an occasion to draw a kind of balance. Since then there has
appeared indeed a rich literature of scholarly contributions to the
understanding of Paul Celan's poetry, and it is entirely justified
to ask first what has been achieved. In their own way, each has
sought—and thought to have found—keys for unlocking this or
that Celan poem. As one of the first readers and interpreters, I
feel a bit strange here. My little book was really the commentary

of a reader who wanted to provide help for reading and who made no scholarly claims.

With respect to art, and above all with poetry, we are of course nearly always concerned with a middle ground between scholarly investigation and direct, comprehending response. It is no accident that literary studies in other countries have completely shunned the name "science" and have been content to call themselves "criticism" or "letters." Of course, this does not mean that poetry is not also subject to the standard of interpretive correctness. One obviously cannot expect to agree on a straight path of progress leading to an ultimately correct interpretation. Nevertheless, young scholars cannot do otherwise than lay claim to their researches as progress, and, in fact, there is a genuine deluge of research methods and results which one can call upon today when it comes to Celan. However, in the first place it is not this perspective to which the history of the interpretation of poetic work like that of Celan's is subordinate. Here the standard of progress in research is not crucial. What today is called "reception aesthetics" carries more weight. Reception aesthetics is concerned with the transformation of the manner of experience itself, with the results of subsequently acquired experience of the world and of art; it is concerned with the change of sensibility and the potential for asking questions which take effect in the receiver. No less important in this regard, especially in Celan's case, is the transformation in the poet's own style, which reflects the tragic curve of his life, concerning which Bevilacqua recently contributed an illuminating study in *Celan-Studien* (volume 2). "Breath-crystal" inaugurates a new style—very short, concentrated poems, a kind of poetry that borders on the cryptic. At the time it left some Celan readers helpless. Some readers accustomed to the *Melos* of earlier volumes of his poetry found no melody in this volume which could bring the unity of the poetic statement to speech. For my own part I followed in those days the path which, as I later saw, the poet himself always recommended: "Just read, read again and again." This cannot have been meant completely literally. Celan himself complained often enough when he encountered misinterpretations that people simply hadn't looked up information in the lexicon. Celan could obviously differentiate between what one can experience by listening to the poem—as

I had once tried through many a long Sunday of meditation in the Dutch sandhills—and what one can and must know. A *poeta doctus* like Celan hardly knows, however, what one can and cannot presume of the reader. That is why grasping for the lexicon is quite understandable.

Nevertheless, one must also ask how much actually depends on it. Perhaps not as much as one might think given our scholarly training. With all the innumerable gains in our knowledge which we owe to new discoveries, we probably don't gain all that much in cases like this. I call upon my own experience. In some cases, there is no question that there were important things I simply didn't know. Thus, in the second edition of my little book I had to correct myself in two instances. In one case it was not I who was at fault, but most likely the printer or the typesetter, whose mistake Celan himself discovered only later— and tolerated calmly. That the text had "heaven's acid" when "heaven's coin" was intended seems to be an incredible difference.* And yet perhaps it wasn't really a printing error, but rather a genuine variation in the text itself. In any case, by either reading my understanding of the poem was not so completely wrong, and so at the time I even let both texts be printed next to each other in the first edition, since the erroneous text with "heaven's acid" was the only one known to many readers.

The second case is one where my own ignorance led to a misinterpretation. I did not know the meaning of "armored ridges" as a technical term in geology, and I had to correct myself later on. Yet here, too, no total reevaluation followed for my interpretation of the poem overall. Just compare page 95ff. in the two [German] editions. It is thus generally true that even when one misunderstands something, if one has been listening carefully, more has probably been understood than if the most exact knowledge had been applied without listening to the poem as a whole. The question arises once again: what must the reader know?

I don't want to repeat myself, and so I refer again to the appendix of the revised edition of my little commentary (pp. 149–53), where I was occasioned by a posthumous essay of

---

*Gadamer discusses this printing error and its impact on his commentary in the Epilogue to the Revised Edition, pp. 154–57 in the present volume.

Peter Szondi to respond to this subject. The question is certainly not: must the reader know everything? It is self-evident that scholarship will pursue whatever can be known. The question is whether the effort to understand a poem, to experience it as a poem, must fail in some cases because one doesn't know something. That is especially true whenever, as is the case with a poet like Paul Celan, the common background of the European cultural tradition completely overlooks an essential element. In Celan's case this is the presence of Jewish mysticism and East European Judaism, in general. Paul Celan's poetic imagination was undoubtedly inspired by both. Of course, one can acquire some background through one's own reading, and so I, too, have read [Gershom] Scholem. But in this respect other interpreters have far more knowledge than I, especially a well-informed reader like Otto Pöggeler, who makes frequent use of this key to the Jewish tradition. In the case of "Breath-crystal," however, I can hardly ever follow him when he brings into play such knowledge. In fact, I find it significant that, like many other readers, I believed myself to have understood well this cycle of poems, "Breath-crystal," without knowing or missing anything from that tradition. I could give reasons why that is especially true of this sequence of poems. I would simply recall the dedicatory poem in parenthesis [page 122].

Pöggeler's distinction between Goethe's symbolism and Celan's allegory does not constitute, in my opinion, a convincing contrast.* What one must or simply can know depends on the type of text. One ought not exaggerate, but with a true poem, one whose form has wholeness, acoustic form and semantic content remain independent from the results of scholarly discovery. One need only think of the degree of understanding which, for example, Mozart's *Zauberflöte* permits for comprehension of the text, or of the "handbooks" of Greek tragedy.

In conclusion, for purposes of illustrating what I mean, let me draw on a contribution about "Thread suns." It seems perfectly clear to me as a reader that the poem describes the great spectacle in the heavens when the sun shines through a cloud

---

*See Pöggeler's discussion of Gadamer's book in *Spur des Worts: Zur Lyrik Paul Celans* (Münich: Karl Alber, 1986), beginning on page 179.

bank, so that, as people say, the sun is "threading" *[Fäden zieht]*, not unlike the opposite expression "*es regnet Bindfäden*" ["steady downpour"]. The learned contribution printed here introduces a scientific instrument, the *"Fadensonnenzeiger."** The author is thereby able to provide literary documentation for the meaning of the word "thread-sun." Thus he does not get the meaning by looking up at the sky or listening to a popular expression. Of course, the parallel shows that the peculiar allegorical explanations offered long ago of the emaciated sun have also become scientifically refutable by the evidence the author adduces. But that the poet, let alone the reader, should have thought about this instrument seems to me to be fully beside the point.

I would thus like to express my thanks for the many things I was able to learn at the conference in Heidelberg. And I would also like to express my wish that interpretive practice make much use of Mr. Neumann's fine contribution at the conference to the concept of song.* It is true that the song quality of Celan's late work no longer appears dominant. But does that mean that we are left with the task of solving a crossword puzzle? For me, in any case, with those few poems of Celan's late period which I really understand completely, the unity of the melody which resounds through the poem as a whole is also unmistakable. With respect to this poetry, aren't we all still merely beginners and listeners? Then one must conclude with Socrates, who made the following judgment in relation to Heraclitus: "What I have understood is splendid, and that will probably also be true on the next go around. Obviously, one needs a master diver to bring the treasure to light."

---

*The pun about the two kinds of threads does not work in English, which has no equivalent colloquial expression. The contribution to which Gadamer refers can be found in Peter König's "Der Fadensonnenzeiger: Zu Paul Celans 'Fadensonnen'" in the Buhr and Reuss collection. König provides illuminating information about the possible origins of the word *Fadensonnenzeiger*, which apparently derives from the Greek *Filargnomen*.

**Neumann's article on song is not included in the Buhr and Reuss volume, but Gadamer discusses the relationship of language and music in "Unterwegs zur Schrift?" in GW 7.259–60.

Index of Names

Adorno, Theodor, 161
Allemann, Beda, 153
Aristotle, 93

Bach, J. S., 171
Benjamin, Walter, 1, 163
Bense, Max, 161
Bernstein, Charles, 44–45
Bevilacqua, G., 185
Billeter, Walter, 58
Blanchot, Maurice, 6, 9, 23, 26, 41,
    45–46, 49
Boeckh, A., 130
Bollack, Jean, 81, 162
Brecht, Bertolt, 31, 146
Brierly, David, 46
Buber, Martin, 128
Bücher, Rolf, 131, 153
Büchner, Georg, 19, 21, 46
Buhr, Gerhard, 46, 182

Cage, John, 36
Calderón, 101
Caputo, John, 49
Cavell, Stanley, 7–9, 39
Cummings, E. E., 39

Dallmayr, Fred, 11
Danto, Arthur, 32–33
Davidson, Michael, 7, 9
Deleuze, Gilles, 18
Derrida, Jacques, 1, 29, 47, 181
Duchamp, Marcel, 1–2, 4–5

Eich, Gunter, 82, 131
Euripides, 101

Fóti, Véronique, 49
Foucault, Michel, 9–10
Fredman, Stephen, 39–40
Friedrich, C. D., 99
Fynsk, Christopher, 43

George, Stefan, 35, 86, 134
Goethe, J., 137, 142, 163–164, 176,
    178, 182, 187
Guattari, F., 18

Habermas, J., 3–4
Hamburger, Michael, 58
Hamlet, 30
Hartman, Geoffrey, 35
Hegel, G. W. F., 37, 42
Heidegger, Martin, 2, 11–14, 20,
    23–26, 43, 47, 172, 178
Heraclitus, 94, 101, 188
Hölderlin, F., 43, 129, 132, 146, 156,
    172, 177, 182

Jakobson, R., 138, 178
Jameson, Fredric, 41
Jesus, 105, 170–176
Joris, Pierre, 58

Kafka, Franz, 18
Kant, Immanuel, 93, 147

189

Printed in the United States
32963LVS00006B/126

9 780791 432303